Transformational Learning
in Community Colleges

Transformational Learning in Community Colleges

CHARTING A COURSE FOR ACADEMIC AND PERSONAL SUCCESS

Chad D. Hoggan | Bill Browning

Harvard Education Press
Cambridge, Massachusetts

Paperback ISBN 978-1-68253-404-5
Library Edition ISBN 978-1-68253-405-2

Library of Congress Cataloging-in-Publication Data

Names: Hoggan, Chad, 1971– author. | Browning, Bill (Consultant), author.
Title: Transformational learning in community colleges : charting a course for academic and personal success / Chad D. Hoggan, Bill Browning.
Description: Cambridge, Massachusetts : Harvard Education Press, [2019] | Includes bibliographical references and index. | Summary: "Transformational Learning in Community Colleges details the profound social and emotional change that nontraditional and historically underserved students undergo when they enter community college. Drawing on case study material and student interviews, the book outlines the systematic supports that two-year institutions must put in place to help students achieve their educational and professional goals. Chad D. Hoggan and Bill Browning articulate the transformative changes that many community college students experience-or need to experience-in order to successfully navigate post-secondary education and launch professional careers. The authors provide a window into the student experience of transformation by drawing on research, theory, and the voices of students. They offer practical guidance on how a renewed focus on student transformational learning can complement the skills curriculum, accelerate current community college reforms, and help lead to higher student success rates in college and careers. The book offers recommendations, classroom practices, and action points that can be integrated systemwide across departments and programs, and tapped by faculty, administrators, staff, and leadership eager to champion student success. These institutional changes, the authors contend, will render the community college a more robust, nimble entity, one capable of supporting students at each critical stage of their academic and emotional development. At a time when community colleges are being called to account for the measurable success of their students-in college and in the workforce-this book is a call to change how they approach their work so that they can fulfill their mission to promote social and economic equity for all of their students"—Provided by publisher.
Identifiers: LCCN 2019025961 | ISBN 9781682534045 (paperback) | ISBN 9781682534052 (library binding)
Subjects: LCSH: Transformative learning. | Community colleges. | Educational equalization. | Academic achievement.
Classification: LCC LC1100 .H64 2019 | DDC 378.1/543—dc23
LC record available at https://lccn.loc.gov/2019025961

Published by Harvard Education Press,
an imprint of the Harvard Education Publishing Group

Harvard Education Press
8 Story Street
Cambridge, MA 02138

Cover Design: Wilcox Design
Cover Image: traffic_analyzer/DigitalVision Vectors/Getty Images

The typefaces used in this book are Adobe Garamond Pro and Milo OT

CONTENTS

FOREWORD

NEARLY TWENTY YEARS AGO I served as the graduation speaker for a small nonprofit training program in the Virginia suburbs outside of Washington, DC. The Training Futures graduating class was made up primarily of New Americans, mostly immigrant women who had come to the United States in search of a better life for themselves and their families. Instead of my delivering the graduation message to them, they gave me a lesson I will never forget. During the ceremony, several described the journey that brought them to that day. Their stories were incredibly inspiring. These adult learners recounted how they had experienced tremendous suffering in their birth countries, faced persecution and discrimination on their journeys to becoming American residents, and often were exploited and abused once they arrived. Many had been beaten down and nearly defeated by these experiences. Then they recounted that through the Training Futures program their lives had been dramatically changed from being that of victims stuck in multiple low-wage, dead-end jobs to becoming competent, confident, and capable front-line office staff employed with company benefits for the first time in their lives! On a college campus, these learners would have been treated as "high risk" students who needed significant developmental education before starting college-level work. But in the Training Futures program, they spoke of how they worked their way through a very demanding and rigorous program while developing job-related basic skills as they went along, how they were supported by a staff who had high expectations and gave high levels of support, and how they encouraged each other through setbacks and tears, learned by doing, and achieved incredible results. In the end, more than 80 percent of those who started the program finished and landed new career-track office administration jobs with higher wages. It was a transformation from poverty into self-sufficiency. Talk about student success! They were the most inspiring graduation speeches that I ever heard.

As president of Northern Virginia Community College (NOVA), I wanted to know more. Were the Training Futures program and its students so exceptional that their results would be impossible to find elsewhere? Could the program's "secret sauce" be adapted and transferred to other settings, including community colleges? Bill Browning, who had been a program leader with Training Futures, joined NOVA with a mission to find out. He identified and defined Training Futures' key practices and documented the program's outcomes. We worked with other community-based organizations (CBOs) in our region and found that several of them, including those that were part of national organizations such as Goodwill Industries and Year Up, demonstrated similar practices and showed astonishing results like those of Training Futures. Bill and I were convinced that program designs and practices like those of Training Futures and others could be adapted and integrated within the community college. He helped to develop several partnerships that creatively combined the strengths of the college with CBO training programs targeted to historically underserved populations and created pathways out of poverty and into employment paying livable wages. The results were spectacular!

A few years later, after retiring from NOVA and joining the Aspen Institute's College Excellence Program and the Belk Center for Community College Leadership and Research at North Carolina State University, I learned that Chad Hoggan, my colleague as a professor at NC State, was one of the nation's leading researchers and writers on what was called "transformative learning"—learning experiences that dramatically change people and their lives. He described to me the theoretical underpinnings and research findings of his work, and that description explained exactly what I had observed in the Training Futures students. I asked, had he considered the potential application of this work to community colleges? Had he ever worked with anyone who had been part of a transformational learning program at a CBO integrated with a community college? He had to meet Bill Browning! I introduced the two to one another, and within a few months the idea of this book was born.

What Hoggan and Browning have produced is a first in community college literature. It is a practical guide to significantly improving learning success in community college programs that is anchored in adult learning theory and validated by research across a variety of fields. Hoggan provides the organizing conceptual framework around transformative learning and grounds the book in decades of research. Browning's years of frontline experience in both community colleges and high performing CBO training organizations brings practice to the forefront. Together they have created a blend of the best of theory, research, and practice to give community college educators a thoughtful and practical guide to transformational learning in community college programs.

Transformational Learning in Community Colleges differs from other contemporary works in how it deals with the subject of improving community college student success. The focus of this work is not on the typical topics of developmental education redesign, course and credential completion, or guided pathways, though these are all critical aspects of any institution's student success strategy. Instead, this book is about significantly improving holistic supports for teaching and learning, a focus that far too often has been missing in national and institutional student success reform conversations. It is targeted to community college faculty and advisors with clear implications for program heads and department chairs. My sense is that much of what the book presents will resonate with faculty and others on the front lines of working with community college students, because it will be validated through their own experiences.

One big takeaway from the book for practitioners is that cohort learning is a powerful design for providing holistic student supports, especially when intentionally designed to create a sense of belonging and mutual accountability. Many of the students' stories and quotes within the book reference the transformative power of peer-to-peer support relationships, and several of the transformational learning methods described in the book are far more effective when used with cohorts of students who have begun to know and trust one another. And, in situations where a true cohort design may not be possible, it can be approximated in ways such as connecting classes into learning communities, as has been dramatically demonstrated at City University of New York's Kingsborough Community College through their Accelerated Study in Associate Programs. "Applied learning" proves to be another powerful and practical approach whether it's through work-based learning, contextualized learning, or simulation. Often learners overcome developmental education deficiencies when they can see how English or math can be applied to real-world situations or are needed in the workplace. Other recommended practices highlighted by Hoggan and Browning, which should be exceptionally valuable to practitioners, include partnering with high performing CBOs and assigning advisors as case managers throughout students' programs, rather than assigning any available advisor, as is too often the practice.

I believe *Transformational Learning in Community Colleges* will provide faculty, program heads, and others who work directly with students with the tools they need to create and sustain transformational learning experiences inside and outside their classes and programs. With this book's recommendations, faculty, advisors, program heads, and department chairs can design and initiate efforts to improve teaching and learning success centered around sets of courses, programs, or clusters of programs without having to remake the entire college. These transformational learning practices, I believe, can be embedded within programs as part of college-wide strategies such as developmental education redesign and guided pathways.

These holistic supports for transformational learning could very well be some of the critically important missing pieces in understanding why so many community college students don't complete the programs they start. And adopting these supports could be the beginning of breaking a cycle of student failure that has plagued many families intergenerationally. I am reminded of a talk I had with some of these heroic graduates one year. I told them (as tears streamed down their faces): You are living proof that the American dream can work, not just for you, but for your children and others in your family and community. They are all watching you. Because if you can do it, so can they.

ROBERT G. TEMPLIN, JR.
Professor of the Practice, Belk Center for Community College Leadership and Research, North Carolina State University, and Senior Fellow, College Excellence Program, The Aspen Institute

INTRODUCTION

*"The rich gamble on the stock market and on property values;
the poor gamble on long shots—lottery, numbers,
and sometimes education."*

—LAST GAMBLE ON EDUCATION[1]

F OR COMMUNITY COLLEGE students, education offers the promise of a future, of being able to provide a living wage for
themselves and their families.[2] For many students, education is
seen as a bridge between two worlds. The world on the far side of
the bridge involves productive and profitable employment, which
usually requires a college degree or other employer-valued credential. It represents stability, respect, and the ability to meet one's
adult responsibilities. It includes being able to participate fully in
the broader social, economic, and civic spheres.

The view of the far side of the bridge, however, can be murky.
Many students cannot fully relate to it because they come from
backgrounds without a college-going tradition. They may have
limited exposure to professional role models or to social networks
that include professionals in their fields of study. The world they
know is too different from the one on the far side of the bridge.
They have adapted to the realities they grew up in, and these adaptations often do not provide access to the other side of the bridge.

The side of the bridge they are currently on is the world of the
economic outsider. This world is the social reality of people who,

for whatever reason, find themselves separated from careers capable of providing a living wage. For these students, the educational process is daunting because it involves more than just gaining a few new skills. It requires a degree of change that can be described as *transformational*. This degree of change involves a type of learning that is different from the acquisition of knowledge, skills, and attitudes commonly referred to when educators discuss course objectives and pedagogical design; indeed, they go well beyond normal curricular content. This type of learning is often referred to as *transformational learning*, and it is extremely challenging, distressing, and emotional.[3] All too often, these needs go unrecognized, unsupported, and unmet. Unsurprisingly, students who are having to navigate these transformational processes have the lowest completion rates.

For students on the economically disadvantaged side of the bridge, the culture, expectations, and language of college are often just as unfamiliar and daunting as the professional world. Especially for those whose experiences in high school or during an unsuccessful run at college left them with the impression that they were not good at "book learning," the prospect of reentering education at a college level is a fearful one, full of uncertainty. These students face a double dose of transformational learning: one as a student in higher education, and the other as a prospective professional in a new career or occupation.

The central argument of this book is that if community colleges pay attention to the transformational learning needs of their students, they will experience a significant increase in student success in terms of completion rates and labor market outcomes, especially among their most vulnerable students. Many individual faculty and advisors who work directly with students intuitively understand these student needs and aspire to support them, but they lack a road map for what such support might look like. These professionals often give Herculean efforts and bring about profound change with many students. We applaud the efforts of these individuals striving to go above and beyond. However, the very fact that they need to go "above and beyond" in order to support students is a problem. The challenge for these professionals is that they are swimming against the current of institutional inertia. They feel as if their focus is supposed to be on academic learning, generally meaning curricular content, rather than these supposed extracurricular challenges. On the contrary, we argue that the transformational learning needs are not extracurricular; they *are* academic learning needs.

While we appreciate the efforts of these advisors and faculty, the process of providing an effective education for all students goes well beyond what the unsystematic, uncoordinated efforts of individuals can ever do. Because of institutional inertia and the often-unmapped challenges of transformational learning, we believe that individual efforts will never be enough to make significant increases in student success. It will require a coordinated effort across the entire community college campus, knowing what students' transformational experiences are like and understanding how others have successfully supported students with these needs within a program of study. It will require each academic program to involve all their faculty and advisors in working together as a team to address, plan for, and effectively support all the learning needs of their students.

Every community college we have ever worked with is already involved in new initiatives, if not in complete overhauls, such as the implementation of guided pathways and the redesign of developmental education. We believe these efforts are necessary in order to make the dramatic improvements in student completion rates that are so desperately needed, but we fear there is a missing piece. As community colleges engage in this curricular redesign, for instance, they need to be sure to address student learning needs holistically, including students' transformational learning needs. A mantra we follow in this book is that supporting students throughout their transformational experience does not require a host of new initiatives and programs. Rather than implementing new programs, our recommendations require community colleges to work within existing structures and processes with an eye toward the ongoing needs of students in the midst of transformational change.

There is no single solution to the challenge of addressing the transformational learning needs of students, nor do we think there are turnkey solutions that will work at every institution—or even in every program within the same institution. Further, the solutions that will work do not necessarily have to be time intensive and prohibitively expensive. What they *do* have to be is systematic. Ideally, solutions would include individual faculty and advisors, programs, departments, the institution as a whole, other stakeholders such as local industry and K–12 systems, and, if applicable, the entire state's community college system. We realize that such a magnitude of change is not likely to happen immediately. However, we believe the ideas presented in this book can help community colleges begin to support students more holistically at any of these levels. They are complementary to existing reform efforts, especially if institutional leaders use our framework to deepen their understanding of the holistic learning needs of all students.

This book takes as its focus the work needing to be done at the program level, as we believe that is where "the rubber meets the road." Any worthwhile change will, of course, have a greater impact when it occurs across the whole institution. However, since most community colleges already have campus-wide change initiatives in place, we feel the missing piece—or starting point—does not reside there. Rather, it resides at the program level, where the curricular design, teaching, and advising of each program are customized for the unique needs and situations of the discipline and its associated career paths, as well as to the unique demographic of students it serves.

In this book we draw examples and inspiration from a program that exclusively targets the most vulnerable students, addresses their transformational learning needs systematically throughout everything they do, and has enjoyed consistently high rates of success. This book also draws upon transformational learning theory—which originated from research in community colleges and is now backed by a large body of research—for insights into what students are experiencing and how transformational change can be supported and facilitated.

This book is written for anyone interested in community colleges (or workforce development and career pathway training programs that enroll similar populations), and in particular for those interested in improving student completion rates and labor market outcomes. It sets out to help community colleges address, plan for, and systematically support the transformational learning needs of their students. Our focus is on faculty and advisors working together at the program level, as we feel this group has historically been left at the margins of conversations about student success.

This chapter presents two challenges that exist as we see them. First, there is the challenge of students whose learning needs include transformational learning. Much of this book focuses on this challenge, its roots, and its manifestations, and we introduce the challenge in this chapter. Second, there is the challenge of institutional inertia or reform fatigue that exists and must be overcome. We present a condensed history of community colleges to explain the causes and effects of this inertia in terms of student success. Then, we introduce Training Futures, a training program that has implemented an approach focused on the transformational learning needs of its students and from whom we draw inspiration and examples provided throughout the book. We then present an overall approach to enacting the types of changes we advocate and conclude with a roadmap for the remainder of the book.

CHALLENGE #1: STUDENTS' TRANSFORMATIONAL LEARNING NEEDS

There is a dilemma inherent in the design of community colleges. Namely, they are intended to promote social and economic equity by providing an affordable education to everyone, including and especially the least privileged members of society. However, their design mirrors traditional universities, which were in turn designed to serve what they regarded as the majority of their students (white, middle-class, recent high school graduates from a college-going family tradition). The typical community college student today is certainly different from that demographic. Many students are some combination of being a first-generation college student, coming from a low-income household, being an adult returning to school, and/or being part of a "racially minoritized" group.[4] The dilemma arises from the mismatch between the purposes and the design of these institutions. The design of community college does not account for—and does not serve well—the least privileged members of society, the very students they were uniquely created to serve. For these reasons, in this book we refer to the student subgroups such as those named above as *historically underserved.*[5]

There are already many calls for community colleges to better serve student needs by changing their design, such as by implementing the guided pathways and developmental education reforms mentioned above. However, even if and when these called-for changes are enacted, the majority of students will still struggle if the very real and powerful learning needs discussed in this book continue to be perceived as extracurricular and remain unaddressed. These learning needs arise because, for historically underserved students, the college experience often prompts or at least contributes to a larger process of dramatic personal transition and change—a *transformation*. We want to emphasize this point by stating it again. Many community college students show up on campus already embroiled in a larger process of dramatic personal change; this change process is likely what prompted them to return to school. For other students, the community college experience will cause them to begin a transformational journey. In both cases, students will be attending classes at their local community college with much deeper learning needs than those most often provided for in classroom learning.

During this time of transformation, students are wrestling with issues of identity, adapting to new demands and social contexts, and questioning long-held understandings about the world, how it works, and their place in it. In short, they are engaged in transformational learning, and not only are these learning tasks difficult, they are occurring at the same time that students are trying to engage in the curricular learning of their coursework. In many ways, students are looking for this personal change; they decide to enroll in community college because they want something different, something more in their lives, with a new and well-paying career often seen as the gateway to a new life vision. Nevertheless, when the challenges of college contribute to this larger and arduous process of personal transformation, more often than not it proves too much for students, and they eventually drop out.

So, what does this look like on a personal level? There are many students arriving on campus who must first confront the fears, anxieties, and doubts that can stop them in their tracks at the beginning of their college journey. These fears show up in conversations with confidants or in self-talk. For young adults who had difficulties in high school, emotional barriers might be articulated in comments like:

> *"I'm not very good at school/tests/book learning."*
> *"I'm not college material."*
> *"My teachers never liked me."*

For older adults who have been out of formal education for years, and especially those who live close to the edge of poverty, the doubts may take a different form, such as:

> *"I'm too old for college."*
> *"I don't have the time or money."*
> *"I can't fit school in with my work and family life."*

For students without a college-going tradition in their families and neighborhoods, college can feel unfathomable, like a foreign country with its own language. This cultural gap might be expressed in statements such as:

> *"I don't know where to start."*
> *"I don't belong."*
> *"My parent/significant other/friend doesn't think I'll make it in school."*

These illustrations are examples of deeply embedded messages and beliefs that new students must confront and change if they are to succeed in college and the careers for which college opens the door. These anxieties and fears may rise up, unbidden, at each difficult moment when navigating college. Most students will have to wrestle to some degree with these fears, anxieties, and doubts, and community colleges will experience greater student success when they are able to help students navigate them. However, as with most challenges, these obstacles fall particularly hard on historically underserved students, who are less likely to have internalized self-images as college students, mentors and role models to help guide them through the college process, or cultural norms that align with those of the community college. For these students, resisting the urge to give in to these worries and give up on college takes repeated and sustained resolve at each encounter.

The institutional practices and norms of higher education favor and cater to students from a specific background: usually white, middle-class, recent high school graduates, whose family members are college educated. We concur with Dowd and Bensimon that when institutional "policies and practices such as recruitment and admissions, student assessment and placement, faculty and staff hiring and promotion, pedagogy and curricular content, and degree qualifications" combine to privilege one group of students and disadvantage other groups, then the institution itself is complicit in maintaining inequity in terms of the graduation rates and labor market outcomes of its students.[6] Therefore, we need to figure out how community colleges can best support all students, including and especially the historically underserved, in obtaining a valued credential so they can gain access to a life-sustaining career. To begin this process, in this book we try to convey the community college experience from the perspective of historically underserved students, so that reforms of institutional policies, processes, and practices can begin with the needs of these students in mind.

As a small but introductory example, following are three typical difficult moments during a student's first encounters at a community college.

- *Transportation and parking*: For low-income students without a car, one of the first navigational barriers is how to get to campus. For example, if a long bus ride is required, this planning step or initial experience may bring to the surface doubts about affordability and having time to fit college into daily life. "How can I afford bus fares on top of tuition, when I struggle to make ends meet even now?" For those with cars, where to park as a visitor may trigger similar doubts. The confusion over where to park without risking a ticket has been known to lead unsure prospective students to give up on college without making it past the parking lot.
- *Testing*: At many colleges, a new student's first step may be taking a college placement exam at a testing center. Such high-stakes exams give rise to test anxiety and intense fears of failure, especially for those with negative experiences with high school standardized tests. The testing center experience at the beginning of the program nearly doomed the first cohort of the Training Futures–Northern Virginia Community College coenrollment program.[7] Only a small fraction of participants placed into college-level coursework. Groups of participants huddled in the hallway outside the testing center, consoling one another, with many of them upset to the point of tears. It required several damage-

control conversations to restore a sense of confidence that they were smart enough to learn applied college coursework. Poor test results tapped into such fears as "I'm not smart enough for college." In later cohorts, when the placement test was scheduled several months into the program, results soared. Even those who scored below college level had already discovered that they could learn and succeed in the program, so the damage done to their belief in themselves was minimal.

- *Counseling*: Students who are unsure of their course of study may be directed to an online catalog to read what may seem like a hundred pages of hieroglyphics. For a student who does not yet know what a credit is, or who does not have any idea what they want to study, this can be daunting. Alternatively, a student may wait in line to ask questions at the counseling center. There, from harried counselors handling long lines of inquiring students at the beginning of each semester, they learn of the often bewildering array of degree and certificate programs, each with its own prerequisites, required courses, and electives—words which may have no meaning for students unfamiliar with college terminology. There is no time for counselors to explain unfamiliar academic terms like transfer credit, AA/AAS/AS degrees, syllabus, accreditation, and the alphabet soup of course code abbreviations. These encounters can reinforce a belief that one does not belong in this world of college.

Evaluating institutional structures such as parking regulations, testing centers, and counseling centers from the perspective of historically underserved students would alleviate some of the barriers to success that community colleges inadvertently place in front of students. But these changes, by themselves, are not enough. They would cut away at metaphorical branches of the problem rather than at its roots. To get at the root of the problem, we need to explore in greater detail the mismatch between historically underserved students and traditional community college structures and practices.

CHALLENGE #2: INSTITUTIONAL INERTIA

Of all higher education institutions, community colleges work with the greatest variety of students in terms of cultural and economic backgrounds and educational preparation. With this diversity comes an equally wide array of learning needs, many of which extend beyond those commonly addressed in course syllabi. There are many community college students whose cultural background is starkly different from the culture on which community colleges are based—the culture they are therefore designed to serve. For these historically underserved students, the community college institution often feels like a foreign environment.

This foreignness has its effects. According to the National Student Clearinghouse Research Center, for students who began community college in 2011, African Americans graduated at a rate that was approximately half that of white students (26 percent vs 46 percent).[8] Similarly, of dependent students from a family income in the lowest income quartile (less than $30,000 per year), only 27 percent completed an associate or bachelor's degree within six years, compared to 34 percent of dependent students from a family income of $30,000 to $105,999 and 38 percent of students from a family income of $106,000 or higher. Although we do not find these statistics surprising, we do find them disturbing. When some groups historically and consistently see less benefit from attending school, we believe it is fair to say that they have been underserved by those academic institutions. And what makes this situation especially problematic is that community colleges are intended precisely to serve these students and to promote social and economic equity.

At many community colleges, several of these student subpopulations are increasingly represented in new enrollments and are likely to rise further, based on US demographic forecasts. A typical college may also be experiencing a shift in its public funding, away from funding based on enrollment and toward more performance-based funding dependent on successful completion rates. As community colleges face a shift in enrollments such that historically underserved students (who consistently have lower completion rates than historically served students) may be edging closer to becoming the majority, and as the institutions' funding is increasingly dependent on successful completion, these disparities may no longer be just a moral or ethical question, but also one of institutional survival. Therefore, if community colleges are supposed to serve the purposes of social and economic mobility, they should be designed to support the learning needs of all students—and especially of their most vulnerable students.

Community colleges are asked to do heroic work that attempts to address a confluence of complex social challenges in the US. Over the first fifteen years of the twenty-first century, colleges have been asked to do more with a steadily declining amount of per-pupil funding in most states. Therefore, one of the principal causes of performance concerns in community colleges is this gap between an enlarged mandate from the public and various levels of government for what the schools should be doing and the shrinking public resources available to work with. Such gaps are especially present in advising and student services. This widening gap can dramatically complicate the challenges of advancing solutions for the specific areas of concern that this book notes. Those same resource constraints also make comparatively lower-cost and high-impact reforms, such as many of the recommendations in this book, a more attractive and sustainable option versus more costly alternatives.

A Short History

The current system of community colleges has its roots in the junior colleges of the early 1900s, which were created to provide a liberal arts general education to prepare students to transfer to traditional universities. Over time there arose a need—thanks to the rapid growth of American industry in the midst of the industrial revolution—to create a skilled workforce in response to new industrial technologies and practices. Traditional four-year universities were not nimble enough to adapt to the quickly changing demands of industry, nor did they have a focus on creating skilled labor. The community college system as it is today evolved from the junior college system and various other approaches to creating a system that could provide an education for students wanting to transfer to a four-year institution, but also an education to prepare students with current, relevant workplace skills.

This evolution was shaped also by American ideals of social and economic mobility. Unlike most universities, community colleges have open admissions policies. In most situations, potential students only need to have a high school diploma or the equivalent to enroll in associate degree programs. Also, tuition is intentionally kept low. By these means, it is hoped that anyone wanting to acquire an education to prepare for family-sustaining employment can gain it at their local community college regardless of their economic situation. Complex problems, of course, are rarely solved by such simple solutions; economic class and other factors still act as barriers for many potential students. Nevertheless, the intention of providing an education for anyone desiring it is embedded in the heart and soul of community colleges.

This ideal of providing access to higher education to everyone led to a focus on expansion. Community colleges sprang up all over the country, and students who otherwise might not have considered pursuing a college degree began enrolling.[9] This focus was heightened by the GI Bill introduced after World War II, which prompted many returning veterans to enroll at their local community colleges, and again by the introduction of the Pell Grant system in the 1960s and 1970s, which made it more feasible for low-income students to attend college. In the resulting rapid expansion, community college campuses (main campuses only, not including satellite campuses) almost tripled from 1949 to 1980, from just under 300 to almost 850.[10] Similarly, total fall enrollment increased from less than one million in 1969 to a peak of over seven million in 2011.[11] In addition, there are currently another five million students per year taking noncredit courses.[12]

This huge influx of new students, combined with low tuition and the colleges' open-access admission standards, had an unintended consequence: community colleges were inundated with students who were not prepared for college-level coursework. In response, community colleges implemented programs in remedial education, adult basic education, and English for speakers of other languages. The intent behind these programs is laudable: if students are not prepared with the foundational skills needed to succeed in college coursework, then the schools must provide a way to prepare them. Historically, the approach has been to assess incoming students to determine if they are ready for college-level work, and if they are not, to place those students in developmental education courses.[13] Therefore, the first encounter many prospective community college students have is at a testing center, where nearly 60 percent of them are told that they are not yet "college-ready" and must successfully complete one or more developmental education courses in reading, math, or writing.[14]

Historically underserved students are, by their very situation, much more likely to be in the group of students required to take developmental courses. These students may be the first in their family to attend college, reliant on federal aid, and working to help support their family. And now they are faced with yet another hurdle—the requirement to complete developmental education—thus depleting limited federal aid on courses that will not even count toward a degree. And, despite the best of intentions in providing developmental coursework, these practices have not worked. In 2010, Thomas Bailey and Sung-Woo Cho reported on data from Achieving the Dream showing that 28 percent of students referred to developmental math did not even bother to enroll, another 30 percent did not complete at least one of their courses, and yet another 10 percent discontinued their coursework even though they had not actually failed a course. In all, only 31 percent of students referred to developmental math finished the course sequence—and only half of those students (16 percent of the original group referred) completed a curriculum-level math course sometime in the next three years.[15] This *successful* group did not necessarily complete their credential; they merely took a college-level math course! We do not have data on how many in this group actually made it to the completion of their credential. In most instances, these developmental education practices actually become another barrier, rather than a support, to student success. And, because historically underserved students are much more likely to be required to take developmental coursework, this barrier profoundly affects them, the most vulnerable students.[16]

This tangent into developmental coursework is just one (albeit important) example of the effects of institutional structures on community college student success for underserved students in particular. It evolved from the community college's focus on providing access to education to as many students as possible. Although this focus sounds laudable, it can be a disservice to students who are encouraged to invest their limited time and money even though data show that the current institutional practices of community colleges do not help them to complete their education. The solution is not to abandon the community college's purpose of providing access to education for all, of course. Rather, we believe the solution is to critically evaluate and reform institutional structures, policies, and practices to match the needs of *all* students. A focus on access is not only inadequate, it is particularly unfair to historically underserved students.

This observation is not necessarily new, as over the last decade there has been increased pressure placed on community colleges to focus on student completion of degrees or other credentials. Helping students succeed in these areas is going to require a fundamentally different approach to supporting student success than has traditionally been done in community colleges.

A TRANSFORMATIONAL EDUCATION

For many students, and especially for the historically underserved, the community college experience not only poses intense adjustment requirements, it also sparks much larger and deeper personal changes. To compound matters, these students often are already embroiled in the process of larger life changes, which may be what prompted them to pursue higher education in the first place. The resulting disorientation holds the potential for profound personal change—that is, transformation. There is a large body of theory and research around transformational learning focusing on the learning needs required of people going through transformational change. We explore this theory in more detail in chapter 1, and we use it as the framework for the remainder of the book. Our premise is that many community college students are experiencing transformation and attending school simultaneously. These students have additional learning needs beyond the technical knowledge and skills for their chosen programs of study. To be clear, we are not disparaging the course objectives listed in syllabi. They are essential. However, they are also not sufficient for many, especially the most vulnerable students. The key question is: How can we support students in navigating their transformational journeys as they strive to complete a college credential and launch a life-sustaining career? Simply put, we need to give more attention where more attention is needed. And if colleges do this well, they will make significant progress toward accomplishing their goals of higher completion rates and labor market outcomes, as well as fulfilling their overall mission to promote social and economic equity.

Throughout this book we offer practical applications for implementing the ideas presented here. Some of these recommendations may seem like such a drastic change from current practices that they are not feasible. To this concern we respond that all the applications presented in this book have been successfully used at postsecondary institutions or other similar postsecondary training programs. Other applications may come across as seemingly trite, perhaps as being too easy to implement to do much good. To this concern we say that even short exercises can have profound and long-lasting effects on students and their ability to persevere through college and, more important, to imagine and believe in new possibilities for themselves and their future. There is great power in symbolic exercises and activities that can influence internalized self-images and habits of mind, which often silently and unconsciously drive behaviors that may no longer serve students well in their new settings.

Another way to view the applications presented in this book is by the type of support they provide. In our process of analyzing the design of programs that support transformational learning, we noticed that there were five specific forms of support interwoven throughout everything those programs did. These forms are: social, practical, inspirational, reflective, and emotional; we use the acronym SPIRE to refer to them. As we present the transformational learning process of historically underserved students, we demonstrate specific ways these forms of support can be provided such that they address specific challenges that are essential for students to successfully navigate if they are to persevere through their community college education.

We are not saying that every community college should implement the specific applications highlighted in this book, nor that if they do their historically underserved students will magically begin completing their programs of study at higher rates. Rather, we hope that this range of practices and supports demonstrates a fundamentally different approach to providing a community college education. The focus in this approach begins with the students, and with a special focus on historically underserved students and their transformational learning needs. If community colleges do this, all their students will benefit. But, since these practices and supports uniquely remedy some important challenges faced by historically underserved students, we expect that disparities between completion rates of historically served and underserved students will decrease markedly.

TRAINING FUTURES

Many community colleges across the country have already implemented practices similar to those described in this book, and we showcase some of them to illustrate that our approach to education, while perhaps radical, is not impossible for community colleges to implement. However, our main source of examples is not a community college. We do this for two reasons. First, we wish to look outside the proverbial box created by institutional inertia, so we have sought insights from an educational program designed for low-income adults and conducive to being applied in a community college setting, but that was not developed within the norms and constraints of traditional higher education practices. Second, we have been able to gather plentiful data, including powerful quotations from students, to illustrate what the transformational journey looks like for students.

Therefore, the career education program that provides the bulk of our illustrative examples is the nonprofit Training Futures (TF) program, which has had great success with students, and its long-running coenrollment partnership with Northern Virginia Community College (NOVA). Material for this book is drawn from this partnership from its inception in 2003 through 2013.[17] Training Futures is a twenty-five-week training program targeted to low-income adults, offered by a regional social services organization called Northern Virginia Family Service in the suburbs of Washington, DC. It focuses on administrative skills such as keyboarding, Microsoft Office software skills, filing, and customer service, with the intent to prepare its graduates for entry-level administrative jobs in healthcare and general office administration. We acknowledge that the initial jobs TF prepares its graduates for are not as lucrative as those that most community college programs aspire to for their graduates. Nevertheless, for these students, these jobs are seen as something beyond what they could have imagined themselves obtaining before beginning the program by providing an entry into professional work environments. Becoming qualified for and obtaining these jobs is a momentous achievement for them. Repeated surveys of TF graduates suggest that the majority of them not only retained their jobs, but also earned promotions.[18] These surveys show continued wage progression to levels that are often double what they earned prior to enrolling in the program. Many graduates also reported gaining access to important benefits such as employer-paid health insurance and paid vacations. These follow-up surveys of program graduates show that many of them have used these entry-level jobs as stepping stones to more lucrative careers, demonstrating that they have learned how to learn, adapt, and grow in their professional development. We believe this is due, at least in part, to their educational experience with TF, which taught them much more than just the skills necessary for entry-level positions. The transformational learning they experienced in TF, we are convinced, allowed them to not only obtain an entry-level job in a new, better career, but it also helped them develop the capability to continue an upward career trajectory.

TF is not a normal community college program. It exists as an off-campus specialized program outside of the typical structure of a community college, but it operates with academic oversight by a sponsoring dean and conforms to accreditation standards. We recognize that this allows TF a degree of freedom that would be difficult for traditional community college programs to duplicate.

However, because of this freedom, TF has been able to design its pedagogy and institutional support with a focus on student success rather than on college norms and precedent (that is, "the way things have always been done here"). For this very reason, we believe it is important to learn from programs such as Training Futures.

Another reason is that TF enrolls mostly "triple nontraditional" students with multiple characteristics that are typically associated with low college completion rates. Participants are mostly working students in their thirties who are supporting families (including many single parents), have low basic skills (averaging around the seventh-grade level for English language abilities), and are from low-income households. The staff for the program, however, employ a strength-based perspective in their interactions with participants, often pointing out characteristics associated with success, such as resilience in rebounding from significant life challenges, high motivation and determination to make a change in their lives, and generosity in supporting their peers in the program.

According to a study published by the Aspen Institute in 2011, TF enjoyed a 94 percent completion rate, an 84 percent rate of graduate employment in new training-related jobs within six months, and an average wage increase of 29 percent in graduates' first jobs compared to their wages prior to initial enrollment.[19] The success of the TF program can be partly attributed to a focus on preparing its students holistically for crossing the educational and professional bridge. This holistic approach necessarily includes students' needs for transformational learning.

What TF did—and what we believe all community colleges will need to do in order to meet the needs of historically underserved students—was to plan in advance for these challenges. They approached these learning needs at the instructor, program, institution, and community levels by integrating activities and support structures specifically designed to help students in the midst of profound personal change. We draw from the experiences of TF, and especially of coauthor Bill Browning's experiences working with TF, to provide examples and illustrations of the challenges that many students face and the systematic ways colleges can help them navigate those obstacles and successfully complete their educational programs. A more complete description of TF is provided in the appendix.

ROADMAP FOR THE BOOK

In the first chapter we introduce transformational learning theory, which provides a research-based approach to understanding deep learning and change. We articulate several specific transformational learning needs that community college students have. We also introduce the ten phases of transformational learning to illustrate what many students are going through as they experience transformational change.[20]

We coalesce these ten phases into three broad themes that serve as the structure for most of the book: tumultuous aspects of transformation, exploring the path forward, and reintegration. In each chapter, we provide quotations and descriptions about what the experience looks and feels like for underserved community college students, as well as explaining what is happening with students. We offer guidance for facilitating transformational learning practices based on the needs and struggles of each phase. In the appendix, we present a case study of the Training Futures program at Northern Virginia Community College. We illustrate how this program successfully designed and implemented a structure to support and facilitate transformation among its students.

This book's contents have been presented in abbreviated form at several community college conferences and professional development seminars. In each instance, attendance has been standing room only, and the level of interest and feedback about the topic from community college audiences has been tremendous. This attests to the fact that professionals engaged in the success of community colleges and its students have an intuitive sense—based on their experiences—that the needs we describe are real. Many or even most instructional faculty and advisors were attracted to community colleges in the first place because of a deep commitment to help change their students' lives for the better. Yet they see large swaths of the student population struggling to succeed in college, and they seem to agree that the only way for significant improvement in student outcomes to occur is for community colleges to critically evaluate and change how they approach their work. In other words, they see the need to transform the way that they work at the college in order to achieve their mission to help transform students' lives.

The goal of this book is to provide a way for these professionals to systematize their work, based on a time-tested theory, research, and the experiences of educational programs that have already done what we are advocating. In this way, our hope is that the Herculean work that many individual faculty and advisors are already doing can be translated into the overall design of academic units and institutions, thus exponentially increasing their effectiveness in improving completion rates and labor market outcomes for their students, and decreasing the discrepancies of these outcomes between their historically served and underserved students.

The good news is that the community college audiences with which we have engaged seem to have a strong desire to help all students succeed. The challenge is the strong inertia of conducting the business of education the way it has always been done. There needs to be a shift whereby community colleges engage students more holistically. This book is an effort in that direction. We offer a roadmap for a common journey that many students experience while at college, a way of understanding and talking about some important needs of community college students that faculty and administrators have noticed but may not have had the words to describe. In doing so, we provide that essential vocabulary, as well as a research-based approach to explaining what is happening with students and practical guidelines to address the transformational learning needs of community college students. The chapters describing each of the three thematic stages that mark students' transformational journeys conclude with ways for readers to explore the themes from within their current roles. Our hope is to deepen readers' understanding of these experiences and identify immediate ways that they can support students during these phases. In many ways, the journey that we present for students is also one that many community college professionals involved in systematic changes or reform also undertake (a process that we highlight in chapter 5). For those who take the risk of letting go of comfortable but disappointing certainty to embark on an uncertain path of significant change toward a brighter vision of what may be possible, we are all students on a transformational learning journey.

1

Defining Transformation

"I'm not smart enough."
"I can't fit school in with my life."
"I don't really like school."
"My teachers always picked on me."
"I don't really deserve any better."
"My (spouse/parent) doesn't think I'll succeed."
"Employers don't really want me anyhow."
"None of my friends are enrolling in college."
*"My family is angry that I'm going to school
instead of working more hours."*

THESE ARE ACTUAL quotes that coauthor Bill Browning heard during his time at Training Futures. In fact, quotes like these are things that he heard over and over again—and anyone who has worked with community college students has probably heard them before as well. It is disheartening, especially because these statements do not have to be true. But these thoughts can become reality if students continue to believe them. This chapter takes a closer look at the underlying reasons why students think and say these things. We will use transformational learning theory as a lens through which to understand what students are going through. But we will also provide real-world examples, through vignettes and quotations from actual students, in order to keep us grounded in the reality of what students are experiencing.

TRANSFORMATIONAL LEARNING THEORY

Transformational learning theory (TL) was developed in the 1970s by Jack Mezirow of Teachers College, Columbia University, based on a large study of women enrolled in return-to-work programs at community colleges across the United States. While conducting their assessments of these programs, Mezirow and his team of researchers noticed that participants were changing in ways that extended beyond the scope of the formal learning objectives of the various academic programs. At the time, the United States was in the midst of the second-wave feminist movement, in which women were challenging the social norms that dictated roles they were expected to perform in society, namely as wives and homemakers. And the women in these return-to-work programs were in the middle of this broad social movement. Mezirow noticed that questioning and going against long-held social norms created a momentous experience of change for these women—one that Mezirow felt could be aptly described as a transformation. This experience was difficult and "an intensely threatening emotional experience," as anyone would reasonably suspect of such a life-changing endeavor.[1]

Mezirow's theory is based on social constructivism, or the premise that each person creates their own reality and interprets their day-to-day (indeed, moment-to-moment) experiences in unique ways, but these ways are shaped by social influences.[2] He called these ways of interpreting experience *meaning perspectives*,[3] which he defined as "the structure of assumptions and expectations through which we filter sense impressions."[4]

These meaning perspectives represent how people know the world, and themselves, to be. They are the mechanism by which people interpret and make meaning of all their life experiences. They determine what people pay attention to and what they ignore, create expectations for what should and should not happen, and affect how someone ascribes meaning to external events, thus creating one's subjective reality out of what one sees, touches, hears, and otherwise senses.[5] In effect, a person's meaning perspectives *are* their reality. The student quotes at the beginning of this chapter provide a glimpse into meaning perspectives within the context of the college experience.

The most powerful (and therefore important) of our meaning perspectives are the ones that are so ingrained, that operate so privately behind the scenes, that we are not even aware of them. These perspectives were developed in childhood, outside of our awareness. We learn them from our closest social contacts, and through everyday experiences as well as powerful, emotionally intense experiences. They are not just a collection of assumptions that we hold loosely and ambivalently, but are encoded (to use a computer metaphor) with strong emotional attachments. Even meaning perspectives that work against us are nevertheless clung to because they are our reality.

> Many of our most guarded beliefs about ourselves and our world—
> that we are smart or dumb, good or bad, winners or losers—are
> inferred from repetitive affective experience outside of awareness.
> Because of such affectively encoded experience each person can be
> said to live in a different reality.[6]

Because they operate behind the scenes, becoming aware of these meaning perspectives is difficult, and changing them is especially arduous. In effect, in challenging one's meaning perspectives, a person is questioning things that seem unquestionable. Mezirow presented transformational learning as a form of intellectual development and a uniquely adult form of learning. Whereas childhood is a time of *formation,* he said, adulthood is a time of *transformation.*[7] Children seemingly soak up the world around them like sponges, developing meaning perspectives uncritically (that is, without deciding whether or not their assumptive structures are true or valid). In contrast, adults can develop the capacity to become aware of, evaluate, and even change their own meaning perspectives. However, the process of doing so is not easy. Because meaning perspectives are developed during one's formative years and are learned from the most influential social figures in our lives, to question one's meaning perspectives can feel challenging, threatening, and possibly even like a betrayal. Humans seem to have an intensely strong tendency to defend their existing ways of understanding the world rather than questioning or evaluating them.[8]

Nevertheless, many adults do go through a process of recognizing, evaluating, and changing their own meaning perspectives. Mezirow called this process perspective transformation, but it has more commonly become known as transformational learning.[9] A useful definition of TL is that it "refers to processes that result in significant and irreversible changes in the way a person experiences, conceptualizes, and interacts with the world."[10] In this definition, the influence of meaning perspectives is apparent. First, they shape how the person *experiences* the world, the way they interpret and emotionally react to events. Second, they dictate how the person *conceptualizes* the world, or how they understand reality to function. Third, they determine how the person *interacts* with the world, including the actions they engage in and how they do them. Hence, transformational learning is not an everyday event; it is a life-changing occurrence that, more often than not, is accompanied by a long period of extreme mental and emotional difficulty.

Despite being first published in 1978, interest in Mezirow's theory really began in the 1990s. Since then, it has become one of the most researched theories in adult education.[11] Yet when we informally surveyed community college conference audiences, asking how many were familiar with Mezirow and TL, very few hands were raised. This theory, although developed in the community college context and well-used and validated in the discipline of adult education, has yet to be commonly utilized in the research and practice of community college education. Obviously, in the decades since its inception, many scholars have contributed to Mezirow's theory. Some of this work is referenced throughout the following chapters of this book.

As an educator, it is necessary to know what you are trying to accomplish in your teaching in order to plan for and enact the desired learning. For the purposes of this book, the crucial thing that needs to be considered is that many community college students are being challenged in profound ways, and these challenges are a double-edged sword. They provide opportunities for transformation that can yield profoundly positive benefits for the students—or they can be the cause of the students giving up and dropping out of college. And the numbers show that the latter is much more common than the former. Readers who work directly with students may have encountered many who stop attending class, miss appointments, and do not respond to calls or emails. They seem to mysteriously drop out of sight with no explanation. TL offers a framework that can help explain such self-defeating be-havior and point to ways that we can assist those students. There-fore, we need to focus on figuring out how to support students through these challenges, so instead of experiencing them as an insurmountable impediment to their hopes and goals, they expe-rience positive, transformational change that helps them accom-plish those goals. To this end, we illustrate some specific ways that successful students have changed as part of their overall transfor-mation. There are numerous ways that people can change, so we offer some illustrative examples of types of change that many stu-dents experience. The following sections discuss five commonly challenged aspects of students' meaning perspectives: identity, personal narrative, self-efficacy, resilience, and social norms/code-switching. For each of these aspects, the potential outcomes of transformational learning are critical to student success in their community college careers and beyond.[12]

Identity

"I'm not college material."

One of the main challenges that many students face deals with their sense of identity. For many community college students, there is a struggle between their imagined future possible self—the person they are hoping to become—and their current image of themselves.[13] When there is a large gap between these images, students tend to feel like impostors as they begin to take steps to-ward becoming their imagined possible self. As highlighted by the opening quotes of this chapter, historically underserved students often feel like they do not belong in college and that other people are looking down on them. This leads to a sense of alienation. Per-haps more important, it can form a barrier to becoming who they want to become. At some point, students need to feel like they are legitimate college students who belong at college. They also need to eventually develop a self-image that is consistent with the professional role they intend to take on after graduation. Until they experience this shift in identity, students are particularly vulnerable to dropping out of college. Educators who are aware of this inner struggle between a student's vision and current reality can assure students that such experiences are normal and encourage discussions of this shared experience to help reduce a feeling of isolation and non-belonging.

Personal Narrative

"I never finish what I start."
"Maybe it's just not meant to be."

We all have stories we tell ourselves, most often based on our life experiences. When frequently told, self-stories become woven into our identities and outlook on life, and they can shape our behavior in a variety of settings. These individual narratives are often adapted from common narratives taught by our culture. They also affect our psychological meaning perspectives, as they simultaneously form and are formed by our self-concepts. For example, if self-doubting quotes like those noted at the beginning of the chapter are repeated frequently—either out loud with others or internally as self-talk—they become part of a student's personal narrative about themselves as learners. When a student arrives at community college weighed down with these stories, fears that they are following a similar script can be easily triggered, interfering with learning and dragging down their confidence as learners to the point where they question whether they should continue to invest in what looks like an impending failure. There is a powerful self-protective instinct to avoid the pain of being evaluated as a failure, so some students avoid this pain by missing class and failing to complete assignments, falling further behind. In the world of employment, such patterns of self-defeating behavior rooted in a sense of alienation and not-belonging are sometimes referred to as "firing yourself." Educators who are aware of this risk can choose to provide extra support and encouragement, point out individual strengths to build upon, and acknowledge that new learning usually comes with challenges. Haven't most educators experienced such a teacher or mentor in our own lives? Students encountering such a mentor are less likely to trigger negative scripts, and they are more likely to use this fresh experience to begin developing a new narrative as capable learners who can rise to meet challenges, learn from experiences, and change the old narratives.

Self-Efficacy

"I'm no good in school."
"I am simply not good at taking tests."

Albert Bandura coined the term *self-efficacy* in 1977 as he sought to fill a missing element in the social learning theories of the time.[14] Contemporary theories focused on behaviors and how they are affected by environmental factors, but Bandura noted that there were important personal factors that affected how people lived, adapted, and engaged in change. One key personal factor he emphasized was self-efficacy, or people's beliefs about whether and to what extent their actions can influence events in their lives. There is a generalized sense of efficacy about every aspect of one's life. However, it is also context-specific; people can increase or decrease their sense of self-efficacy in particular parts of their lives. We are focused specifically on students' academic self-efficacy—the extent to which they feel that studying and other efforts will help them learn and succeed in school. Many community college students have developed low academic self-efficacy, especially those who had less-than-positive experiences in high school or have previously failed at college. Therefore, when learning challenges inevitably arise, it can be difficult for them to persist; at a deep level they do not believe that their efforts to learn will matter. Helping these students increase their academic self-efficacy greatly increases their odds of successfully completing their community college education.

Resilience

"I'm afraid of failing again, so I don't try hard."
"I can't do it because I'm disabled."

Resilience refers to one's ability to adapt well in the face of adversity, trauma, threats, or other sources of significant stress.[15] Recent brain science studies have found that people living on the edge of poverty are weighed down by constant stress, which diminishes their resiliency. According to Elisabeth Babcock, those who grow up in poverty are "likely to be hypervigilant, more focused on survival and the immediate future, more worried, distrustful, less able to make and follow through on plans, and have a harder time anticipating the thoughts and behaviors of others and interacting with them."[16] For low-income community college students, such effects can quickly turn into a cascading sequence of course failure, loss of financial aid, and becoming another dropout statistic. Whereas scholars used to assume that resilience was an innate and unchangeable trait, it is more commonly seen now as something that can be developed and improved.[17] College can be a challenging experience for most students, but it is especially so for the historically underserved. In addition to all their other learning requirements, these students are also having their resilience tested, and are engaged in the introspective work of trying to learn from their challenging experiences, thereby (perhaps unknowingly) developing an increased capability for resilience. This, of course, is exhausting work. Educators who are aware of these threats to resiliency can respond with curricula that give opportunities for early learning successes, and anticipate and work to mitigate risks when coursework becomes more challenging.

Social Norms/Code-Switching

"I'm not college material."
"My family doesn't see the value of education."

For historically underserved students, encountering the academic language, expectations, and social environment of college may feel like setting foot in a foreign country without knowing the language, the culture, or any other people. For example, one Training Futures student, after being informed that they could also earn college credits while in the program, asked, "What's a credit?" These students will be learning an entire new vocabulary and set of rules and expectations in order to succeed in college, and they may undergo the painful experience of feeling like an outsider as they ask questions that everyone else seems to already know the answers to. For some students, their home or neighborhood cultures may have mocked or dismissed college-educated outsiders for being too book-smart, lacking common sense, or even as being oppressors; they might feel conflicted about cultural assimilation into college as an act of betrayal of important people in their lives. Educators can explain to these students about code-switching, or learning new social norms and how and when to switch between newer social norms and habitual ones. Code-switching is an important adaptive skill for everyone to practice in order to relate to people outside of their home communities. Consider, for example, teaching the interviewing skills of making eye contact and describing your past employment successes in responding to interview questions. Many mainstream Americans are familiar with these expectations and can pick them up readily with a little practice. But, for instance, if you are from Ethiopia, as many Training Futures students have explained, you were taught from a young age to always avoid eye contact with strangers and to always be modest and humble, never bragging. Because of these deeply embedded social norms, learning this new behavior is far more difficult, and it may feel like disowning important teachings of one's elders. Many historically underserved students will come with diverse cultural traditions. Code-switching is a skill that is useful for anyone engaging in multiple, dissimilar social contexts, but it is not always an easy skill to develop.

THE EFFECTS OF THESE UNMET LEARNING NEEDS

These five frequent challenges to students' meaning perspectives (identity, personal narrative, self-efficacy, resilience, and social norms) interact to create a mutually reinforcing negative feedback loop, especially for historically underserved students. Transformational learning seeks to reverse the direction of the feedback loop from a downward spiral of doubt-driven self-fulfilling prophecy into an upward spiral of transformational change. If the direction is not reversed, however, how might this dynamic manifest throughout the student experience and within the college?

- *Identity*: Students who identify as "not college material" may feel their doubts are confirmed by low placement test scores and conclude that they don't really belong in college anyway. It is not difficult to see how this might result in a decision not to register for recommended developmental education courses. When aggregated across groups of students who struggled in high school, or who had a previous failed attempt at college, this dynamic may explain some of the drop-off in registrations following initial enrollment and placement testing.
- *Personal Narrative and Self-Talk*: Students with past struggles in formal education and negative self-talk about their ability to be successful learners in postsecondary education may be less likely to start college. This individual decision, multiplied by many students with similar fears, can help explain proportionately lower college enrollment numbers for many underrepresented student groups.
- *Self-Efficacy and Resilience*: Students who come to college with a history of academic performance struggles may become quickly frustrated with challenging assignments that trigger their anxieties about school performance. With frustrations and fears swirling in their minds, they may lose their ability to focus on assignments and give up, resulting in the assignments not being completed. When questioned, the student may offer other excuses to hide from the shame of being judged as a failing student, and an instructor or

advisor hearing a string of excuses may begin to lose confidence in the student as well. Several such frustrating learning experiences—compounded by unintended lack-of-confidence messages from college instructors and advisors—may further erode a student's academic self-efficacy and willingness to persist, leading to attendance problems, course incompletions, and drop-outs. When aggregated across many similar cases, this part of students' downward spiral can lead to low college persistence rates for historically underserved student groups.

- *Identity, Self-Efficacy, and Social Norms*: Students with a self-image of being "no good at book learning" may quietly believe that no amount of effort can change their fixed identity as a poor student. Someone holding that belief would be less likely to seek out available campus supports, such as faculty office hours, tutoring services, or the writing center; they don't expect that further effort or coaching will improve results, and think that it may instead lead to further embarrassment once others discover that they are "not smart enough." A student who isn't exposed to open and candid conversations about students' struggles may conclude that he or she is the only one with these problems, and therefore shy away from interacting with other students so as not to be discovered as a college imposter, disconnecting them from potential peer support relationships. Beyond campus, if they are among the first in their family and neighborhood to go to college, they may have no one in their close and trusted circle of family and friends to help them. Disconnected from campus supports and without a personal support network of their own to turn to, such a student would feel increasingly isolated, with a heightened sense of not belonging, and they might retreat altogether from campus, letting go of the hopes and aspirations that led them to college.

These examples of common student experiences illustrate how these challenges are connected together in a negative feedback loop for the student. From a college administrator's perspective, however, the experiences of hundreds or even thousands of these students are likely to be visible only as data points in a half-dozen separate reports. Using these separate and isolated data reports without a deep understanding of the student experiences and decisions that drive the data risks embarking on reforms that achieve only marginal improvements, like treating symptoms without fully diagnosing the underlying condition. We believe that TL provides a useful framework for more deeply understanding student experiences. Used in combination with disaggregated data about historically underserved student groups, TL can inform more holistic, student-centered changes in teaching and learning, advising, and college administrative processes that have a greater chance of producing stronger gains in student success.

TRANSFORMATIONAL LEARNING THEMES AND PHASES

When we refer to transformation, we mean that a student is likely to be navigating a series of difficult changes, such as the five described above, at the same time. Any one of these changes is a difficult process of self-discovery and adaptation; dealing with multiple changes at the same time amplifies the difficulty. Many community college students are coping with these learning needs and, at the same time, sitting in the classroom trying to accomplish the course's learning objectives, or roaming the campus trying to determine how and where they need to engage in their unfamiliar surroundings. This is the additional curriculum that is tacitly expected of historically underserved students. If community colleges are to fulfill their purpose of providing an education that leads to a life-sustaining career for all their students, regardless of social and economic background, at some point they are going to have to address these needs as an important dimension within curricula and support services.

This book articulates the challenges and transformational changes that many community college students experience as they strive to achieve their goals. To provide structure, we draw upon Mezirow's ten-phase depiction of the process of transformation. To be clear, Mezirow never claimed that the process of transformation fit neatly into ten phases. Rather, he described the process as iterative and messy. We believe that these phases represent common types of experiences, rather than a rigid, lock-step process for people going through transformation.

However, ten phases is a lot to keep in mind as one considers how to translate TL into new teaching and support service practices. For this reason, we have grouped them into three larger themes: tumultuous aspects of transformation, exploring the path forward, and reintegration (see table 1.1). The three chapters that follow will outline these three themes and discuss related research and student experiences within each.

In each chapter, we provide quotations and vignettes from actual Training Futures students and graduates to demonstrate from a student perspective how these challenges and changes typically manifest with students. We draw upon a variety of scholarly literature to further explain what is going on in the minds and lives of these students. Based on these explanations, we offer specific

TABLE 1.1

Transformational Learning themes and phases

Theme I	Tumultuous Aspects of Transformation
Phase 1	Disorienting dilemma
Phase 2	Self-examination with intense emotions
Phase 3	Critical self-assessment
Phase 4	Recognition that others have been there
Theme II	**Exploring the Path Forward**
Phase 5	Exploring options
Phase 6	Making a plan
Phase 7	Acquiring needed knowledge and skills
Theme III	**Reintegration**
Phase 8	Trying on new roles
Phase 9	Building competence and self-confidence
Phase 10	Reintegration into one's life

examples, drawn from the structural supports and pedagogical methods of Training Futures and other similar programs, of ways to help students navigate the difficult transformational learning process. We also suggest immediate actions that readers can undertake to explore students' journeys in each phase, in order to deepen their understandings of the student experience and identify ways that they can support them.

2

TUMULTUOUS ASPECTS
OF TRANSFORMATION

THE FOLLOWING STORY is from a vocational education teacher in Arizona.

A young woman in a composition class came to ask me about the class. From what I said in our first class and in my opening materials, she gathered that I expected thinking, creativity, honesty, and enthusiasm. I answered "Yup." She said she could not do those things. I answered that those things happen in many forms, and that she did them all the time in other parts of her life, so we could just make the transfer to the class, and I was there to help. She told me I did not understand. If I gave her endless workbooks to fill out, or lists to memorize, or copying to do, or errands to run, she could pass the class, but I could not ask her to think. She could not do that.

Without reflecting on what I was about to say, I asked, "Who told you you were stupid?" She answered without a moment's hesitation, "Mrs. Butler in the third grade. Wasn't she right?" [. . .]

"No," I cried to that student, "Mrs. Butler was wrong. She had no right to tell you that. Did you like her? Did she like you? Were you friends?"

She answered, "No, she hated me."

"Then why do you want to give her the power to define you and your life? Ever since you came in here, you have impressed me with your intelligence. In fact, you explained your lack of creativity very creatively. We can work on anything you need. You can do this, and if you need more time, you can have it." And on and on, *and she didn't come to our next class.* [emphasis ours]

I have cried "NO" to Mrs. Butler and the system, the premise she represents, ever since, in the memory of that student and all of us like her.[1]

We are all products of the environment in which we were raised. For better and for worse, we develop our most baseline meaning perspectives during our formative years. These patterns of behavior and thinking, as well as a sense of who we are and how the world works, become deeply ingrained, and the process of evaluating and changing them is profoundly emotional. As educators, we do not (and indeed cannot) force transformation to happen. Our role, rather, is to create an environment that supports and facilitates change for those students who are experiencing enough disorientation that they are ready and willing to engage in the process of transformational learning. We find in the above story a reminder that transformation for students does not automatically happen just because we as educators hope for it, plan for it, and teach for it.

For this student, the instructor's first class obviously caused enough discomfort to make her seek him out.[2] As do many students, she chose to drop out of the program rather than persist in the face of her doubts and other challenges to her educational journey. It may be that she was simply not at a place in her life where she was ready to engage in the difficult processes that might propel her toward a positive, life-changing educational experience. Or maybe the professor or the institution could have done something more to help her deeply engage with a productive self-examination rather than running away. This is one of the eternal dilemmas of education, and of course there is no clear and easy answer. However, if community colleges are going to reduce educational disparities, we need to understand this part of the educational process for students. This chapter explores the various tumultuous experiences common during transformation, and especially during the beginning of such change: a disorienting dilemma, self-examination with intense emotions, critical self-assessment, and recognizing that others have been there.[3] For each of these experiences, we offer a practical application for how community colleges can support students through it. Toward the end of the chapter, we provide several more applications that could support one or more of these experiences. The concluding section of the chapter provides suggestions for immediate actions that readers can take to deepen their understanding of the tumultuous parts of the transformation process and identify ways that community college professionals can support students within their specific roles.

DISORIENTING DILEMMA

When someone's life experiences do not align with the expectations based on their meaning perspectives, it causes discomfort. It represents a threat to reality as they know it. Often, one can simply ignore these instances and move forward with one's life without engaging in the mental and emotional work of change. However, sometimes this discomfort can build to a critical mass that inspires transformational learning in individuals. Indeed, for major personal change to occur, there needs to be enough discomfort to provide motivation to engage in the difficult work of deep learning and change.

Mezirow refers to the discrepancies between reality and one's meaning perspectives as *disorienting dilemmas*. These dilemmas cause a general state of confusion, dissonance, angst, and/or discomfort that can build to a critical mass and propel the person onto a path toward transformation. We find disorienting dilemmas to be a quirky academic term that perhaps downplays the upheaval that people go through. It fails to really capture how dramatic, indeed traumatic, the experience can be. In short, disorienting dilemmas are caused when a person has experiences that contradict their views of themselves, the world, or simply how things are supposed to be. They can be brought about by major life disturbances or by an accumulation of small discrepancies between reality and one's meaning perspectives. Mezirow explained it like this:

> [E]stablished patterns of thought and action become dysfunctional, "trying harder" in old ways does not work and we become compelled to redefine the problem. Transformations can result from such major dilemmas or from the accretion of transformations in related specific beliefs or meaning schemes. Thus a series of insights over several months about how a woman is oppressed by specific sex stereotypic role expectations can lead to a perspective transformation just as such epochal dilemmas as being confronted with the death of a mate, a divorce or a separation might lead to a transformation.[4]

Pause with us for a minute and think back on your life. Can you remember times when someone important to you challenged some of your deeply held beliefs—perhaps beliefs about yourself, your close relationships, your religion, your political stance, and so forth? And when this has happened, were there times when you felt deeply threatened by those challenges, which may have first shown up as a racing heart and a burst of anxiety, fear, or anger? Even when negative beliefs about ourselves are challenged, people tend to feel threatened by the more positive potential beliefs. We consistently justify our current ways of making sense of the world, including negative beliefs about ourselves. And when somebody challenges that, it can feel deeply, deeply threatening.

If you work directly with community college students, especially with adult students who have had more life experience, you might also pause to reflect on their stories. Think of students who have spoken about what led them to start college. Perhaps it was an injury or illness that led them to conclude they needed a less physically risky career. Some may have lost spouses, siblings, or parents, which led them to reevaluate their lives. Many Training Futures (TF) students who were recent parents spoke of going back to school because they felt they were not the role models or income earners that their children needed. Many low-wage working adults return to college in order to break free of the daily struggles of living close to the edge of poverty.

The impetus for transformational change does not always have to come from negative experiences or challenges to existing beliefs. Sometimes it comes from an "integrating circumstance."[5] These experiences are much more drawn out; there is a long period of exploration during which people are searching for something missing in their lives. They may not even realize they are searching for something, but at some level they feel like there is something missing, like a piece of a puzzle. Then, an experience or insight occurs that seems to make things click. As a result, they rapidly start experiencing changes in how they see themselves and the world around them. Many TF participants have cited a new relationship as the impetus for seeking changes; they may not have felt change was possible before a new spouse or significant other person in their lives suggested that they could do more with their lives or careers. In these situations, Clark says that people are experiencing an *integrating* rather than *disorienting* experience. For community college students, this kind of integrating experience may come when a difficult field of study suddenly makes sense and they excel in their coursework, or they discover an unexpected new career field with an advisor that seems to be a perfect fit. Presumably, the changes resulting from an integrating experience are much less traumatic than those caused by disorienting experiences, but we feel it is safe to assume that people in these situations still embark on a series of deep changes with phases similar to those of people for whom the beginning was marked by a disorienting dilemma.

We have been talking about meaning perspectives being challenged in two ways: another person can challenge them by offering alternative perspectives, or life experiences that do not align with them can create an implicit challenge. The latter tends to be much more powerful, and is thus a more common impetus for transformational change, because in most instances that lead to truly dramatic positive change, the level of disorientation must be pretty severe. This realization led coauthor Chad Hoggan to conduct a study with a group of breast cancer survivors. The study subjects had been in remission for several years, and they claimed that, although difficult, their cancer experiences had ultimately made their lives better in some important ways.[6] Even acknowledging these benefits, and after years had passed, some experiences were still raw for these participants. Their disorienting dilemmas were a far cry more than just disorienting; they felt devastating. As part of the study, participants talked about their cancer experiences and what made them so difficult. This question yielded some of the most intriguing findings from the study—findings that are particularly relevant for our discussion here. Even though there is a fairly standard list of challenges and concerns common among breast cancer patients, the study found that for any given participant, there were only one or two that were especially problematic. And for those one or two concerns, dealing with them was overwhelming. For example, one participant talked about how cancer destroys any sense of being in control of your life. Many participants mentioned this challenge, but for this one woman, feeling out of control was unbearable. In her words, it was "horrible, horrible, horrible" until it got to the point where she realized that this challenge was not going to change anytime soon. And at some point, it became so unbearable that something clicked, and she just let go. Five years later, she was laughing about it, saying that for her whole life the need to be in control was a big problem. She had to control everything, and it hurt her relationships and her ability to enjoy life because she felt that everything had to work out just the way she wanted it to. Now, she said, she has lost that need. Her view now is that she is alive; she is good; life is easy.

This process—of traumatic and unwelcomed life crises evolving into valuable learning experiences—showed up over and over again. The particular challenges varied for each participant, but what was consistent was that cancer and its related challenges magnified those issues to an almost unbearable level. Many of them said that if they could have avoided these particular challenges at any cost, they would have done whatever it took to avoid them. However, they could not escape or avoid them. The women in this study—all of them—at some point "let go" or otherwise found a way to change so that these painful experiences caused them to grow and develop in very positive, life-changing ways.

These findings are particularly relevant for our discussion of historically underserved students. First, it is important to remember that the various challenges of community college will affect students differently, but for any given student, one or two concerns may stand out from the rest as being particularly difficult. However, whereas the breast cancer patients described above had no choice but to deal with the challenges of cancer, these community college students *do* have a choice, and that is why we see so many of them drop out of school. Therefore, community colleges need to recognize that it is not lack of willpower or an accumulation of small concerns that causes students to forego their education. Rather, it is often because one or two challenges are, for whatever reason, uniquely and acutely difficult for the student, and these challenges are perceived as being so difficult because they are interacting with some aspect of the student's meaning perspectives that is not serving them well in their pursuit of education. If we can help the student identify and work through those one or two challenges, we will see that, just like the women in the above study, the process of handling those challenges will often yield extremely positive, life-changing learning outcomes for the students.

Causes of Disorienting Dilemmas

We have noticed a few different forms that disorienting dilemmas take. One form happens when students' transformations are part of what prompts them to return to school. Often, there is an accumulation of experiences that leads to a feeling of being stuck, causing a problem for people who want or expect a better life. Consider, for example, the way that Gladys, a thirty-something participant who scrambled for years to make ends meet for her family, introduced herself to her new peers on the first day of the TF program: "Living poor in America slowly beats your dreams down. I came to Training Futures to lift them back up." Of course, if people like Gladys expected their lives to be what they currently are, then they probably would not think of themselves as being stuck. Rather, they would just think, "This is life. This is just how it is." What causes discontent with one's current life situation is the expectation that life could and should be different. Students like Gladys return to school because they have a vision for a different and better life and career, and they see a college credential as the path forward toward their image of what they hope their life will be.

Most of the research literature of transformational learning uses the premise that people have experiences that do not match their expectations (based on their worldview, their notions of self, and the like). We believe, however, that there are variations that are important to consider when thinking about community college students. One variation is when people have a self-concept that says they will never succeed, and yet they have a desire for a better life. There is a conflict between some of their assumptions about themselves and their desires.

Kristy spoke at her TF cohort's graduation ceremony and shared the story of how she came to feel trapped by life events. As she began telling the story of her journey to a roomful of 125 guests, tears welled up in her eyes. "Today is overwhelming." She turned around to collect herself at the podium before continuing. Kristy then described the breakup of her marriage, followed by her husband's illness and death, and the struggle to care for their children as a single parent. "We all try our best to avoid potholes. But I was stuck deeper and deeper as time passed . . . My universe collapsed and I was broken into pieces . . . I felt like a frog in a deep well. I couldn't jump out." At a focus group conversation two weeks later, Kristy and many participants in her cohort described various life events that led them to similar feelings of being trapped and limited in the life choices available to them, with few resources to help them dig out. One said, "My friends told me: 'You can't even pay the rent, what are *you* going to college for?'"

This notion of being stuck came to Kristy's attention because she had an image or an expectation of a better life. Her life experiences built to a critical mass that caused disorientation because the "stuckness" did not match the expectations of her hopes and dreams. We have heard many adult students use the word *stuck* in explaining their decision to return to school. They simply cannot seem to escape the hard edge of living near poverty, and that limits their perceived options to break free, in effect shrinking their world over time. For many, this contrasts sharply with a strongly held vision of a life with greater possibilities. At some point, the worsening tension between this hopeful vision and a (seemingly) hopeless reality reaches a tipping point, leading to a decision to make changes, which in turn often leads someone to return to school. So when a community college educator hears reference to a feeling of being stuck (or some variation) from a new student, the student is likely experiencing some form of a disorienting dilemma. Acknowledging this dilemma signals that a student is likely to be highly motivated to learn, but she may also be vulnerable to anxieties and fears that could serve as impediments to her success in school.

There are also many examples among students of unexpected or sudden life events that force them to deal with dramatic changes in their lives, such as the death of a loved one, divorce, illness or injury, job layoff or termination, legal troubles, the birth of children, and so forth. Consider Goitom, who described the downward spiral that led him to enroll at TF. He is a refugee, originally from Ethiopia, who fled to America in search of a better life. But he found that his lack of cultural knowledge about life in the US was a huge barrier to this vision.

> Whenever I tried to get a job, I couldn't. I didn't even know how American businesses operate. I knocked on so many doors to get a job, but at each and every office after an interview, I was a failure. I became an island. My three children and my lovely wife depended on me. I had to tell my spouse to make new arrangements to eat only once a day. The time selected was 1:00 p.m., to be our breakfast, lunch, and dinner.

Another form that disorienting dilemmas take is when the school experience itself causes disorientation. For historically underserved students, disorientation can arise from such things as the norms and practices of higher education, the demands of college-level coursework, or simply feeling out of place. A strong and supportive new relationship with an instructor or advisor may challenge previously held views of educators as "out to get me" or punitive, prompting the student to reevaluate themselves as learners. But a negative initial experience with college, such as not passing a college placement test, or the confusion of not knowing how to navigate campus, can trigger an intense feeling of not belonging or not being smart enough, leading a student with a powerful self-preservation instinct to flee from this fear and from the campus environment.

Consider a recent study that explored the experiences of students at a two-year college who were required to complete pre-curriculum or developmental coursework because of their low scores on standardized tests.[7] This study focused only on students who had successfully completed their developmental coursework and transitioned to full enrollment in curriculum courses. In other words, it was looking at success cases in hopes of better understanding how the students experienced their coursework. One of the findings we find especially intriguing is how the majority of the study's participants described their experience of finding out that they would be required to complete developmental coursework, an experience that clearly qualifies as a disorienting dilemma. They recounted feelings of being rejected by the college and being isolated from their peers. It was more than being embarrassed by being classified as inferior to other students, or being frustrated because it was going to take them even longer to graduate. It was a blow to their identity and to the imagined future person they were hoping to become. The students had just graduated from high school and gotten accepted to college. They were on a high, and proud and motivated about where they were heading in life. Then they were told that they were not good enough to be with their peers. Many of them reacted poorly. They admitted to causing distractions in class and avoiding homework so that they would not look like they were trying too hard. The combination of being placed in a lower, non-degree-counting course and trying but failing would simply be too much to bear. For most of the participants in this study, this reaction turned into a self-fulfilling prophecy, and they failed their first (and sometimes second and third) developmental course.

These particular students described eventually having a wake-up moment, getting serious, and passing their pre-curriculum courses, but most students in their situation do not. They get discouraged and eventually just drop out of college.[8] The challenge of community college professionals is to figure out how to support struggling students when they are experiencing this disorientation, seeing it as a potential trigger for learning and change rather than as a sign that the students have some type of flaw or do not really care about their education. Indeed, the behavior described above is a demonstration that students do care about their education, but that they are reeling from some of the shocks of the educational process. Change is always difficult, and therefore the impetus to engage in making change often needs to be even more compelling. As educators we need to recognize when students are going through this crisis, this disorienting dilemma, so we can support them. However, we also need to realize that this discomfort has tremendous potential for the kind of learning currently being required of these students. It is not that we need to try to make the disorientation go away, but rather that we need to allow it to happen in a way that promotes learning and growth without being overwhelming or working to students' detriment. In the end, sometimes students need to struggle while they let go of previous habits and beliefs that no longer work for them, but they need to do so in a way that supports their learning and growth rather than impedes it.

At a TF anniversary event several years ago, Beatrice, a TF alumna, shared her story about the need to move beyond one's previous concerns in order to create a new future.

My native country is Burundi, but because of ethnic discrimination, I grew up as a refugee in the Congo. When war started in the Congo, it was through miracles that I escaped death, starvation, and homelessness and came to the United States. I am a citizen for the first time in my life.

Training Futures is a miracle in my life. This program has given me so many important skills. But there is so much more. When I came to Training Futures, my cup was half empty. As soon as I started the program, the same cup was filled with love, dignity, security, home, and hope, as well as the business skills needed to succeed in a job that can support my family.

I want to tell you a story that I have remembered so many times in my life. One day, as my mom was returning home from the market, she saw a group of small children standing around a ditch. She went to the children just in time to see a two-year-old little girl fighting for her life; she was drowning in muddy, dirty sewer water that runs in deep ditches by the roadside. [My mother] put her basket of food down, not worrying about who might steal it. She only wanted to save the small child. My mother picked up the drowning child and did mouth-to-mouth resuscitation, not caring at all about the dirty sewer water the child had swallowed, or the smell. She sucked everything out of the mouth of the little girl and then took the child to the clinic for treatment. The child was saved. When my mother returned to the place she had left her basket, no one had stolen the food she had purchased to make lunch for her own children.

From this story, which I have carried with me all my life, I have learned that to be a hero —we need Love and Hope. We must look forward, not back. Whenever we want to make a change in our own life or help someone, we only have to set aside our basket: our basket of burdens, of bad memories, of deception, of doubts, our basket of depression. Training Futures tells us to put our basket of burdens down and step forward. We can create our future.

Beatrice speaks to the need to let go of some of our previously held perspectives and thought patterns in order to move forward to create a new and different future. This difficult but essential process of letting go is seen in many of Mezirow's phases. The dilemma described in such hopeful terms by Beatrice nevertheless illustrates an inner struggle between holding on to the comfort of beliefs, habits, and relationships that are familiar, or facing the fear of trying on new ones that are unfamiliar and uncertain.

This is why it is so important for community college professionals to understand the challenges students are going through. Students are rarely in the enviable position of being able to focus exclusively on learning the course material. As described in chapter 2, they are very often also enmeshed in the process of extremely deep and difficult personal change. It is important to take a holistic perspective on students' educational experience, and to recognize that it includes both course content and the overarching process of intense personal change. From this perspective, the learning needs associated with personal change *are* academic issues. And, as can be seen in this chapter, this process of deep learning and change brings with it intense feelings of discomfort, frustration, and/or despair. It is important to understand what this emotional state looks like in students so that systems can be implemented to support them through the beginning phase of their transformational processes. The activities described in this book, although seemingly simple, can be powerful because they harness the power of imagery and symbolic action. They are designed specifically to address the two primary sources of disorienting dilemmas for historically underserved students: one, the student has a vision for a life better than what they have known or have recently experienced, or two, the community college experience itself is causing the disorientation. In both cases, students are experiencing discomfort and dissonance. There is only a vague sense of a new reality that will relieve this sense of disorientation. Therefore, it can be helpful to provide a mechanism to help students clarify a vision of their future selves and goals, let go of things that are holding them back, and focus on their reasons for pursuing a college education in the first place.

Activities/Supports

One way to support students during their disorienting dilemmas is through activities such as the Comfort/Discomfort Zone ("Inner Pig"). At the end of the first week of the TF program, there is a workshop on the costs and benefits of life changes brought about by participation in the program. The students brainstorm all the "uncomfortable" effects that they have experienced that week by changing their lives to include a twenty-five hour per week training program. The students list things like getting less sleep and getting up very early, hurrying unhappy children off to school or day care earlier than before, experiencing the stress of commuter traffic or public transportation, sitting for five class periods per day, and (for many) going straight to work after the program ends each afternoon. The instructor draws a box around the list to demonstrate that what was "outside the box" or uncomfortable this week will over time become "inside the box" or part of students' comfort zones and engages participants in a discussion about their experiences in adapting to changes. This same discussion process is repeated after the beginning of other phases of the program, including internships, job searches, and finally preparing to start a new job, with the student's comfort zone box growing each time to include new experiences and challenges.

By repeating this discussion when faced with changes, students can become more comfortable with the discomfort of change as a normal feeling that they are prepared to handle. The benefit is more growth, expanded choices and opportunities, and a better career with family-supporting income. During these discussions, the enemy of the process is introduced with humor. This countervailing force pushing back against change is each student's "inner pig," because a pig only likes food and sleep. The inner pig will oink (complain) loudly when pushed out of its small comfort zone and must be put back to sleep until the process of building a bigger comfort zone ends in a payoff that even the inner pig can agree with. Though everyone laughs, the metaphor of the pig comes up in conversations throughout the training as a dynamic that has to be confronted and "put back to sleep."

Student Testimony

"I was a waitress all my life," said Linda, a program graduate speaking as part of a panel to current students in the TF program. "I was working at a restaurant called 'The End of the Road.' I felt like I was at the end of my road, that I would grow old still a waitress. . . . I had reached the age of forty-nine. It was a turning point for me. You see, forty-nine is the age when my father died." Following her recognition of this multidimensional disorienting dilemma, Linda described her experience being in the program: "I worked full-time in the evenings when I was at Training Futures. I was so devastatingly tired. I would fall asleep driving home and have to slap myself to stay awake." Later during the discussion, she revealed that she now earns twice as much salary as she did in her previous job. She was able to tell her story to current students while smiling and laughing, but she emphasized to them that it was no laughing matter when she was going through those struggles. Nevertheless, she said, her sacrifices paid off handsomely.

Stories like Linda's serve as important reminders to students that they can indeed make it through their educational programs and achieve the career outcomes that prompted them to embark on their current journeys. These stories send a valuable message to students about their immediate personal concerns at a time when they need to hear that message—even if only a few in the audience need it at that moment. These messages remind students that other people have been through a similar journey and have been successful despite the challenges. At a time when some students are experiencing a profound sense of isolation caused by their current transformational experiences, messages like Linda's remind them they are not alone and that they can indeed be successful.

SELF-EXAMINATION WITH INTENSE EMOTIONS

Disorienting dilemmas can build to a critical mass and prompt people to take a serious look at themselves and how they are making sense of the world. For many community college students, this process may feel especially acute when the initial exhilaration that carried them through the early challenges of school begins to fade. Just when the newness and luster of recent life changes dim a little bit, and they are facing increasingly difficult challenges in their coursework, students are simultaneously being hit with the intensely emotional experience of looking inward and seeing conflicting, contradictory parts of themselves. There are those parts that are familiar—who they used to be—as well as the new parts—who they are becoming. This inward look can be confusing, especially when different aspects of who they used to be and who they are becoming are starkly different, as is inevitable in significant change.

Jennifer Garvey Berger talks about this phase of transformation as the "edge of knowing," which she writes is "the most precarious—and important—transformative space. It is in this liminal space that we can come to terms with the limitations of our knowing and thus begin to stretch those limits."[9] Several authors have talked about liminality in the transformation process. Kaisu Mälkki and Larry Green, for instance, describe liminality in terms of being the space where old meaning perspectives no longer work, but new ones have yet to be developed. This space, they say, is charged with "edge emotions," such as "anxiety, depression, or other related feelings when our earlier beliefs, attitudes, or values become problematized or when we are not able to understand situations based on our previous experiences, or, when our relationships or acceptance from significant others become questioned."[10]

These edge emotions can vary by individual. Often there is a sense of fear. Because students are beginning to see the world differently, they see a different world around them: a new, scary world that is presenting them with challenges that they are unsure they can meet. Ways of thinking, being, and acting that have helped them adapt to the environments they grew up in may not be of much use in this new world of college and professional workplace settings. And students recognize that they are becoming very different from who they have been in the past. So they are not even sure they know themselves anymore. The newness of everything that may at one time have felt exhilarating can become terrifying. Most students try to hide it, but deep down many of them are experiencing a profound sense of fear: fear of the unknown, fear of who they are becoming, fear of not being able to meet the challenges facing them, and so forth. Some students react to this sense of threat with anger; other students respond with anxiety and/or depression. Some may quietly walk away from their studies, and college faculty, advisors, and administrators may never know why.

During the third week of a TF cohort some years ago, one participant named Susan wrote an SOS note on the back of an evaluation form following a workshop on self-esteem: "Every time I have tried to better my life, something negative always happens. Please help me!! I can't hide it no more." After reading her note, the staff hustled to talk with her, and they arranged an appointment with a counselor to help her address the intense emotions that she had been hiding. Six weeks later, Susan was in the audience when another participant, Dolly, spoke during class in a very quiet voice to announce that she had just been diagnosed with a learning disability, and that she might need to drop out of the program, since learning new material was so difficult for her. Susan met with Dolly afterward in the lunchroom and told her, "You can't quit. You need this program." Then Susan reminded Dolly to remember what she *does* have: "Hey, at least you've got a home. I'm homeless, and I'm still coming in every day." In the days following that conversation (and similar conversations with other peers), Dolly's response to her doctor's prognosis changed from despair and giving up to a new determination to succeed. Susan and Dolly teach us that heroes on a transformational journey may find that they are asked to make a choice whether to confront or shrink and hide from their challenges.

Other common emotions are guilt, shame, or even self-loathing. Students look at themselves, for instance, and wonder how much of their disorientation is a result of their personal flaws. They begin to question things that, deep down, they feel are not supposed to be questioned. This questioning can feel like a betrayal of their most intimate relationships.

While acknowledging students' intense emotional reactions during this phase of self-examination, one might conclude that students need a therapist, not a community college professional, to help them navigate it. There may be some students who could benefit from this, and hopefully many colleges now have a referral resource on campus or nearby for these more extreme cases. However, it is important not to pathologize a natural human learning process. College faculty, advisors, and administrators who are aware of these reactions can reassure students that meaningful learning often comes with an emotional reckoning, that these feelings are normal.

In challenging deep-seated assumptions about themselves and the world around them, students cannot yet quite comprehend how things might be understood differently. This is what we mean by *liminality*. It is an in-between space that is intensely uncomfortable because old ways of making sense of the world no longer seem adequate, but new ways have yet to become fully formed. This experience can be incredibly frustrating, and it is not difficult to understand why some students might choose to avoid the certainty of the present feelings of anxiety and drop out, rather than to take the risk of stepping forward further into an unfamiliar and uncertain new space and place. Truths (with a capital T), once considered absolute and universal, are lost and often can never be regained or replaced except with truths (with a little t), which are relative, tentative, and situational.

Sue Scott aptly described this aspect of the transformation process as mourning, and she says that grieving the loss of one's old self and that self's ways of seeing and being in the world is an important part of the transformational process.

> The person perceives a loss of something familiar in the past that was integral to the constellation of his or her life. This kind of loss compels humans to react in several ways. . . . [It] requires individuals to take time to settle with what is experienced as dissolution. . . . This is not easy work, nor should it be attempted in isolation from support. The work is hard, painful, and it makes one quite vulnerable.[11]

In Nancy Schlossberg's transition theory, she describes this phenomenon as responding to a threat to one's identity and having to manage the intense stress, strain, and emotions that arise.[12] People have to let go of some of their previous roles, routines, relationships, or assumptions. This letting go, she says, involves pain, loss, and a difficult adjustment period during which there is a profound sense of disorder; it is stressful and requires time to process through it.

It is important to understand that during this stressful time it is common for people to engage in coping strategies that minimize the full emotional impact of their sense of loss and disorder, such as using denial- or avoidance-oriented thinking and behaviors. For community college students, this might appear as students skipping class and not doing homework, despite growing evidence that their academic efforts are not proving adequate to learn the course material. Even when students are earnestly trying to pay attention in class, powerful emotions can make it extremely difficult to concentrate and remember. When this happens, students often quit trying to pay attention and tell themselves that they are simply not good at learning. These reactions are understandable, and they can even be beneficial as they help people detach from painful emotions while they might be too intense. However, as students advance further in a course or program, these responses of avoidance and denial will eventually hinder their ability to navigate ongoing transitions and adaptations into evolving new environments and settings.

Activities/Supports

This "intense emotions" section comes with a warning to faculty and advisors to appreciate the limits of their roles and to identify professionals in the college or in nearby community-based organizations to whom they can refer students whose needs for emotional support and guidance go beyond their training and expertise. We do not suggest that faculty and advisors should become social workers or professional counselors. However, students come to classes and advising sessions with emotional responses to the stresses and changes brought about by college programs of study, and faculty and advisors need to engage those students with some understanding of their experiences and provide assurances that some of these stresses are an expected and normal part of the learning journey.

As described in this chapter, many of the students' emotional responses during the transformational learning process come with a negative valence, such as fear, anxiety, doubt, shame, self-blame, and confusion. However, there may also be moments of high energy and joy that students experience during this tumultuous phase. Students may experience moments of clarity as new learning sinks in and their perspectives begin to shift. They may experience joy in rediscovering an interest or ability that had lain dormant. They can form strong and satisfying new connections with people, including faculty, advisors, and other students, and see themselves interacting in new ways that give them hope. These positive moments are cause for acknowledgement or even celebration, while the more challenging emotional responses call for various forms of support and encouragement.

So, how do we support students through these intense emotions? In some cases they need individualized counseling. The TF program includes a weekly visit by a licensed social worker, with whom trainees can sign up for an appointment (often referred by program staff) to discuss their emotional journey with a trained professional, and possibly get referrals to local social programs if an ongoing need for support is identified.

Some colleges have partnered with local social service agencies to provide on-campus mental health services that operate in a similar way. One example is the partnership between Wake Technical Community College (WTCC) and North Carolina State University (NC State), both in Raleigh, North Carolina. In this arrangement, NC State places a student from their Clinical Mental Health Counseling master's program who has already completed between one and three semesters of coursework to serve a practicum on WTCC's campus.[13] There, they provide 120 hours of direct counseling services each semester for free to WTCC students.[14]

For more standard cases, where students do not need a trained counselor, one exercise that can be helpful for students wrestling with these emotional experiences is the Letting Go balloon exercise. Several weeks into the TF program, students are encouraged to jot down on a small piece of paper an old habit, fear, or belief that they need to let go of in order to be successful. They are each given a helium-filled balloon and are directed to tie the note to the balloon. The whole class goes outside and releases their balloons simultaneously. Once back inside, the instructor invites students to share what they need to let go of and what they need to do in order to change these patterns. This activity employs three mechanisms of change. First, it helps students reflect on and articulate one particular way of thinking or acting that is holding them back from accomplishing their vision of change. Second, it draws on the power of symbolic action by prompting students to physically let go of this unwanted habit of thinking or doing. Third, by engaging in this activity in a group, this activity reinforces the message that the student is not alone in her or his transformational journey, that fellow students are also struggling to engage in deep learning and change.

Student Testimony

Midway through the twenty-five-week program, several TF alumni arrived to talk about their experiences at TF. Susan Craver (a cofounder and instructor with the program) moderated the panel. She asked each alum to recount fears, challenges, and accomplishments at TF, and observed aloud that "challenges and accomplishments always go together."

Marie, a graduate from five years previous whose photo recently graced a regional business magazine cover article, began her story by encouraging trainees: "Something great will come of your sacrifices today." She asked trainees to raise their hands if they were having problems learning the computer. Many hands shot up in the air across the room. Marie nodded her head and continued. "I struggled to learn computers, too. I thought that I wouldn't be able to get a job because I didn't know computers well enough. But the more that I played with it, the better I became. If you let it, fear will control you, so you have to put it behind you, and you will overcome it."

Raylene spoke last. She was the most recent alumna, completing TF just three months earlier. "My biggest challenge was

Toastmasters, doing what I'm doing now, speaking in front of people. I'm still nervous." She said this with a strong, clear, voice and confident presence that seemed to refute her words. Despite her intense fear of public speaking, Raylene wants to be a trainer, and she had started a customer service job with one of the world's premier training organizations. "I helped carry others' challenges here at Training Futures. We helped each other. When one of us had a problem, we all came together like a family to help."

In discussing the alumni panel the following day, participants identified fears and challenges that these program graduates had to overcome in order to succeed.

- "A foreign accent is not a barrier to success. You can still go far."
- "You can be nervous and worried about speaking up in groups and still improve."
- "You can rely on the support of staff here to overcome fears and take some risks."
- "We can help each other when someone falls short."
- "I should keep trying on the computer until I get it."
- "The sacrifices and adjustments here will open up doors to success."

CRITICAL SELF-ASSESSMENT

At some point during the personal transformation process, problematic assumptions about ourselves and the world around us are brought to light, and a critical assessment of these assumptions can help people progress through their change process. By "critical," we mean that we not only become aware of problematic assumptions but that we engage with them; we assess them to determine if we really believe that these assumptions accurately portray realities we have experienced, or if they are just an unhelpful remnant from a few key life experiences that diverge from what we have since experienced to be true.

This assessment can be informal and individual, as when someone simply wonders how their views have been wrong. However, it is much more effective when done with other people who can function as "critical mirrors" to reflect our views back to us and help us challenge them.[15] This interpersonal interaction helps us see potential distortions in our worldviews and internalized self-images. One great (and sometimes terrifying) aspect of working in education is the power we have—through faculty and staff interactions with students, as well as institutional policies and procedures—to shape the assumptions that students have about themselves. We can provide positive experiences that, for instance, help students realize that their negative self-images are unfounded, or we can make comments or enact procedures that belittle students and instill or reinforce negative assumptions. Here are some actual quotes, heard in the hallways or classrooms at TF and similar programs in community colleges, that illustrate some ways these problematic assumptions show up with students.

Last year, we threw away an old computer that was messed up. Now, after [the instructor] showed us how computers work, I realized that I could have fixed it.

Sometimes problematic assumptions are about seemingly minor things. In this case, the assumption revolves around something very specific: if a computer breaks, you have to throw it away. The realization that a computer is not an incomprehensible magic box but something that can be understood and, when necessary, fixed is not necessarily transformational in itself. However, an accumulation of these realizations can lead to a deeper understanding about what one can and cannot do to affect change in one's life.

> *I don't have confidence in myself. That's my big problem. When it was time for a raise, I didn't present a case, but just signed off. All I got was twenty-five cents. Afterwards, I felt belittled because I didn't speak up for myself.*

This student is remembering a specific instance (not advocating for herself when due for a raise), how it made her feel (belittled), and an underlying issue (lack of confidence) that she feels is contributing to the problem. The higher education experience can prompt some students to start feeling more empowered and responsible for their lives, which can help them see some of their habitual perceptions and responses. This, in turn, can lead them to learn about other ways of being in the world, such as presenting a case for why they deserve more money rather than passively accepting small raises.

> *I'm realizing that it doesn't work for me to be fearful of others or shy here [on campus]. I need to let go of things that hold me back.*

Here we see a student starting to make the transition from just realizing something to seeing how they want to change. Of course, just because they say they want to change does not automatically make that change happen. Nevertheless, it is a start. Being fearful and shy in educational and professional environments is not necessarily an assumption, per se. Rather, it is a way of being that is tied to a certain context (school, in this instance).[16] Whether an assumption or a way of being, students can still become aware, assess truthfulness or desirability, and then proceed to try to change.

You saw things in me that I couldn't see for myself at the time.

This quote speaks to the power that positive reinforcement can have for students. It shows them a way of perceiving themselves that is different (and hopefully better) than their previous self-image. This type of "positive mirror" comment has been made by many graduating students in numerous cohorts to TF staff. It's also a great reminder that student strengths that seem obvious to college professionals may not be visible at all to some students. Living day-to-day with few resources can lead to a diminished self-assessment that is readily apparent to staff at the start of the program. Such self-assessments trickle out in students' comments that focus more on negative qualities. As participants experience learning achievements and receive encouragement and affirmation from instructors and peers, staff frequently hear more balanced self-assessments that also acknowledge assets and strengths that seem to have been hidden from participants' view in their previous mindset.

Activities/Supports

Engaging in a critical assessment of one's assumptions is an important part of the transformation experience. This is true for administrators, faculty, and staff as well as for students. As educators, for example, we might have developed assumptions about what good teaching is based on our own experiences in introductory courses in college. Ignoring all the contextual nuances of those experiences (perhaps being a highly motivated student, with a background of educational success, brimming with confidence and excitement), we may have made generalizations assuming that all learners will benefit from the way our instructors taught us during those classes. We may assume the need to carry the metaphorical torch of our discipline by continuing to teach the same way we were taught. Yet sometimes we encounter students or situations that challenge these assumptions about good teaching, especially when what worked for us is not effective in helping these students learn. The same scenario happens with community college students: early educational experiences may have led them to create generalized assumptions about learning and about themselves as learners, such as being "bad at math," "not good at book learning," and so forth—assumptions that are not necessarily true and that are definitely not helpful. It behooves everyone, then, to periodically pause and reflect critically on their meaning perspectives that might be causing problems.

An example of how students can be supported through this process of critical self-assessment is the Quote Conversation exercise, as described in this actual classroom example (from TF). Before the Customer Service class starts, the instructor selects a quote and writes it on the white board. Students know the drill; this happens several times a day as each new class begins. Each student takes out a journal provided to them for this purpose and writes the quote down.

"Let us never fear to negotiate, but let us never negotiate out of fear." (Franklin Delano Roosevelt)

"Let's get underneath the words," the instructor says. "What are the key words in this quote that stand out for you?" Students respond by suggesting three words in the quote: negotiate, fear, and never.

"OK, let's look at the word *negotiate*." The instructor wants to take the quote apart and fully explore the meaning of key words, so that these words bring new meaning and fresh energy for students. "What does that mean to you?" she asks the group.

In a flurry of language, the responses fly rapidly from students' mouths onto the white board, where each new word is written in a column underneath the heading "negotiate":

- compromise
- advocate
- trade or haggle
- give and receive

She talks briefly about each word that students suggest, embroidering each one with new meaning before they can be stitched back into new patterns within the full quilt of the quote. "I realized recently that the word 'compromise' literally means 'come to a promise'" is one of the comments. Stepping back from the white board to admire the students' words, the instructor turns, smiling at the group. "Move over Mr. Webster, because you guys have really gotten the meaning here!"

Next, the instructor conducts the same exercise with the word *fear*. Again, new language flies across the room and onto the white board. There are twice as many responses to *fear* as there were to *negotiate*. This is a word with which students have lots of experience. Soon it's time to stitch these new word patterns back into the full quote. "Let's look back at the full quote again," the instructor says as she repeats the quote: "'Let us never fear to negotiate, but let us never negotiate out of fear.' What happens if you negotiate when you're afraid?"

Karen, a student, then states with authority, "It's a human right to speak for yourself. If you don't stand your ground, you lose control and become depressed. You're helpless. You give your power away and sit like a wilted flower waiting to get stomped on." Erika chimes in, too, about how hard it is to translate new philosophy into action. "Negotiating is a part of life. Each one speaks their side, like when buying a car. When I see this up on the board, it seems easy. But it's not. A lot of women especially have this problem." Deborah adds her wisdom to the group. "Fear keeps you from talking about the issues. If you're afraid, you can't make a good decision. Your reasoning is gone."

The instructor shifts attention back to the quote on the board to reexamine this new quilt of meaning that the group has woven together. "Let's compare the first half of the quote to the second half. What you've said is that when you negotiate out of a place of fear, you give your power away. When you do this without fear, you are standing in your power. So, how do you use this in your life?"

Now that new patterns of behavior have been discussed by the group, the group turns to the task of deciding how to put this belief into action. In a fast-paced dialogue, they explore together how to employ these insights in salary negotiations, consumer purchases, even driving a car along congested roads.

These kinds of quote conversations occur for six to ten minutes at the start of each TF class, four to five times each weekday. Many of the quotes relate to attitudes, values, and beliefs needed for success. By hearing others' varying interpretations of what quotes and terms can mean, students have opportunities to reassess their own ways of thinking about life. The quote conversations dialogue sequence—getting at the meaning underneath the words, assessing varying emotional responses and interpretations, and exploring multiple options or ways to apply this philosophy—roughly mimics much of the sequential TL framework. Multiply this short activity over a sixteen-week semester of skill-building courses, and there are more than 300 such conversations that participants experience at TF. Susan Craver refers to this process as "quotes bombardment." Through this repeated activity, students become more adept at consciously assessing their previous assumptions, interpretations, and responses together with a cohort of peers. This activity teaches students the skills of critical self-assessment and provides an opportunity for them to practice until, hopefully, it feels natural.

RECOGNITION THAT OTHERS HAVE BEEN THERE

In addition to feeling threatening and scary for those going through it, the process of personal transformation can also feel intensely isolating. This section explores the social aspect of transformation, the value in recognizing it as a shared experience, and some possible applications to help students make this realization. Consider the cases of several adult students in the TF program. Ghenet's daughter pleaded with her each day when she left for school, "You're not going to class again, are you?" She wanted her mommy home. As you can imagine, her pleading tugged on Ghenet's heartstrings and challenged her commitment to do what it took to finish the program. Same with Viola. "But this is Mom's time," insisted Viola. She shared her response to this plea: "I'm going to call a family meeting. I'm very determined. Nothing will stop me from succeeding [in this program]."

As Craver explains, "Trainees are getting daily reinforcement here, but the family back home doesn't." Dramatic changes by one member of a family or a community often cause others to resist the change. This is a natural response. But it causes students who are undergoing transformation to often feel tugged in two directions at once. By pushing forward with their changes despite resistance, students create temporary relationship friction with family and community members who pull them back toward the familiar.

One way of countering this backwards tug is to introduce new students to successful program alumni whose stories can help pull them forward. When a TF student achieves their goal of a new professional career-path job, that success is celebrated with a ceremony—described more fully later in the chapter—that starts with the audible ringing of a bell. At that distinctive sound, everyone knows to assemble in the office lobby to celebrate a peer's achievement. On one occasion, the bell summoned participants to celebrate the achievement of a former student named Gladys; she had returned to share her story of how she was able to turn down three job offers before accepting the one she wanted. Her inspirational story of success helped new trainees push forward with a reinforcing message: "If this trainee did it, so can I!" Several trainees noted that this particular ceremony gave them renewed hope.

Along with a wide range of other emotions, many students are likely to experience a profound sense of isolation caused by their current transformation. One cause of this is that most are progressing down a path they have never experienced, thus leading to a sense of uncertainty. As described previously, our meaning perspectives are formed by the interaction with—really, social immersion in—our families and the communities in which we grew up. Questioning these meaning perspectives means a lot more than merely finding a better way of seeing things; it is questioning the previously unquestionable. This questioning is deeply disconcerting because, at the least, it explicitly distances us from our most important social world: the family and community of our formative years. Students who are experiencing change that is dramatic enough to be considered transformational are inevitably questioning things that they learned from their most important social figures. They are treading new ground; even if they have role models to look to as exemplars, they are still going to feel acutely uncomfortable questioning old assumptions and trying out new roles.

Immersion into the social milieu of higher education and its unfamiliar norms will likely cause many students to start feeling some discomfort, especially as they start to develop new meaning perspectives based on their experiences in college. One form of this discomfort is a sense of isolation, as students no longer feel completely at home in the social contexts of their youth nor in their new contexts of school and work. It is common to hear community college students say that they do not feel like they belong in college, or that they are not "college material." Comments such as these, we believe, result from a sense of dissonance caused by the unfamiliar environment of college.

Not only do many students begin to feel alienated from their origins as they attend community college, the very process of questioning and changing deeply held meaning perspectives also distances them from their most important social relationships. Significant relationships can be strained because of the dramatic changes students are undergoing. Stephen Brookfield calls this phenomenon *cultural suicide*, which he defines as being "excluded from the culture that has defined and sustained [community college students] up to that point in their life" because they begin to question "conventional assumptions, justifications, structures, and actions."[17] Claiming that a common theme in the autobiographies of community college students is the risk they face when engaging in any kind of critical assessment of the norms of their social group, Brookfield describes the phenomenon in greater detail:

> The student . . . who was formerly seen by friends and intimates as "one of us" may be seen as having betrayed, or left behind, his or her peers. The critical thinker is viewed as taking on airs and pretension, as growing "too big for her boots," or as aspiring to the status of intellectual in contrast to her friends and colleagues who feel they are now perceived as less sophisticated creatures. The learner who has come to a critical awareness of what most people take for granted can pose a real threat to those who are not on a similar journey of self-discovery, or who do not see themselves as engaged in the same political or intellectual project. In the eyes of those left behind, the critically aware student is perceived as having "gone native," or having become a full-fledged member of the tribal culture of academe.[18]

Often, the discomfort of transformation is made worse because people feel as if their experiences are unique—that they are alone. Robert Kegan poignantly described this aspect of the transformation process as "the human wrenching of the self from its cultural surround."[19] One of the most powerful experiences that helps someone progress through their transformation is gaining a sense of belonging. This sense of belonging is twofold. First, it involves the recognition that the disorientations experienced and the discomfort felt during transformation are not unique to them; when people recognize that others have trod this path before, it is as if a weight is lifted from their shoulders. Second, it involves a feeling of recognition, of acceptance into a new social group that aligns with the changes they are making. We offer a few explanations here that resonate with us based on our experiences with students undergoing transformations.

First are the psychological threats to identity that are common during transformation. As part of their psychological and sociolinguistic meaning perspectives, people carry with them a collection of identities based on their affiliation with the various social groups in their lives. Each person has identities associated with, for instance, their race, nationality, religion, gender, socioeconomic status, political affiliation, and so forth. We do not, however, hold all of these social identities with the same amount of importance in every moment. At any given point in time, the salience of each identity varies based on the situation. Sadly, there seems to be a tendency to focus on the social identity that we perceive to be most stigmatized in the particular context we are in at that moment.[20] So when people find themselves in a new context that employs new and unknown meaning perspectives, their foremost identity is often the one that they feel is least valued by the new social environment. Not only does the person feel isolated because of the changes they are experiencing, they often feel devalued in their new and uncomfortable social environment. A new community college student, with limited previous exposure to a college campus or experience with college students, may feel that they do not belong or "are not college material," perceptions which can lead to even further isolation.

The new environment, especially as perceived by a newcomer who feels isolated and devalued, contains numerous situational cues that pose a psychological threat. Take, for instance, a research study of undergraduate students in math, science, and engineering (MSE) majors who watched an MSE conference video.[21] Some participants were shown a gender-unbalanced video, wherein members attending the conference were mostly men, and other participants were shown a video where conference attendance was gender balanced, comprised of equal numbers of women and men. The female participants who viewed the gender-unbalanced video exhibited greater cognitive and physiological vigilance, shown by such indicators as faster heart rates and greater increases in skin conductance, suggesting a perceived threat. They also reported a lower sense of belonging and less desire to participate in the conference. The female participants in this study seemed to focus on their gender identity, presumably because of the historical depiction of MSE as a male-dominated field. Consistent with our claim above, foremost in their minds was not their identity as strong math students or as part of a particular religious or political affiliation, but the social identity—gender—that they perceived to be stigmatized in the social context of the video they watched.

These research participants illustrate how feeling marginalized or devalued can have real effects: physical, mental, and emotional. Imagine how these effects might be intensified if their sources extended beyond just watching a video (such as the women in this MSE study). Other research has shown how subtle social cues that communicate to students that they do not belong can inhibit academic performance and undermine motivation.[22] An understanding of this phenomenon can be used to promote positive transformation experiences for people. Motivation, for instance, can be markedly increased by being intentional about providing social cues that help students feel a sense of belonging in an intellectual community.[23] Linden West writes of the deeply creative, relational nature of personal transformation. It requires:

> good enough spaces between people: a sort of neutral area where anxieties can be managed and it feels safe enough to take risks.

Experiments with self, including with the stories we tell—about who we are, have been and might be—can take place. In such processes, the response, encouragement, and understanding of others—a kind of emotionally attuned recognition—are essential.[24]

Because transformation often means that we are changing things about ourselves that we learned from the most important authority figures of our childhood, the process can feel like we are venturing where no person has gone before. Therefore, there is power in recognizing that what you are going through, others have gone through before you—that although you are becoming less like the social group with whom you were raised, you are becoming more like another social group that you aspire to join. West continues:

> When, for instance, the taken for granted is shaken, we may hold rigidly to existing ideas and relationships and retreat to the culturally and cognitively familiar. We may struggle to play with new ideas because they threaten our sense of who we are and make the wrenching of self from context seem unbearable. . . . And yet the good enough instructor or fellow student, in coming alongside, and through empathic understanding, encouragement and giving time, can contain such primitive anxieties and allow some space to process new and radical ideas.[25]

This recognition is a normalizing experience. By this, we do not imply that their experiences should be considered less difficult because others have been through something similar; rather, we are saying that this recognition helps the person see that their transformation is actually a symptom of being human, not a symptom of being odd or deviant from the norm. Other people, including many who come from the same background and social norms, have also changed in dramatic ways through a similar process.

Historically, the modus operandi of higher education is to offer courses and have students register independently for the ones they need. This system is inherently isolating, with few structures in place to bring fellow students together or ensure that they are likely to see the same classmates in more than a single course. The issue is especially problematic for the majority of community college students, those who commute and attend part-time, because they have fewer opportunities to associate with fellow students around campus than full-time students do.

This isolation may not cause problems for some students, but for historically underserved students, who are more likely to be experiencing profound changes, a system that promotes isolation runs counter to the goal of helping them complete their educational program and thereby accomplish their hoped-for career goals. Community colleges need to find ways to provide more social support. One way to provide this is to build it into the design of the educational program, an approach that we call Structured Socializing. For instance, using a cohort system, where students move through a prescribed sequence of classes with the same classmates, allows students to gain some continuity with fellow students. By seeing and working with the same students over multiple courses, students are more likely to build relationships with their peers. As we have seen in the examples from TF, the peer support community that arises naturally within a cohort can be a powerful force for learning, persistence, and success. In nearly every TF cohort, participants who come to know and trust each other provide services such as academic mentoring and tutoring, transportation services by forming carpools, note-taking for students who have to miss a class, and other forms of support and encouragement. TF graduation speakers often attribute a significant part of their success to the support from their peers. College faculty who desire to encourage conversations about common student experiences such as those described in this book will find that the sharing of experiences in classes will naturally lead students to connect with one another and build peer support systems.

In situations where a cohort system is not viable, it is still possible to create a structure that brings students together in meaningful ways. For instance, students can be required, as part of a program or for full course credit, to attend regular meetings with other students in the program. One highly successful nonprofit organization that partners with Austin Community College in Texas, called Capital IDEA, organizes weekly support group meetings for historically underserved students during their first semester. They call these V-I-P groups, which stands for Vision, Initiative, and Perseverance.[26] In other variations, groups may be comprised of all students in the program, all students entering a specific program in the same term, or some subgroup of students. These meetings can fulfill multiple purposes, such as providing forums for learning and social support that are not easily provided in classroom contexts.

Another example is Accelerated Study in Associate Programs (ASAP), a holistic community college reform initiative pioneered by the City University of New York (CUNY) to help more students graduate more quickly. ASAP requires students to enroll in college full-time and to take developmental courses early, in order to graduate within three years. High expectations of these students come with high levels of personalized support. ASAP students have an ongoing relationship with an assigned advisor whose lower caseloads allow for relationships to develop; they also have access to enhanced tutoring and career advising, additional financial support to address gaps, and participation in special sections of college success courses reserved for ASAP students. A three-year study focused on low-income ASAP students who were advised to take developmental education courses showed that, by the end of the study, 40 percent of the ASAP students had graduated, compared to 22 percent of a control group of similar students who were not part of the ASAP program. At that point, 25 percent of ASAP students had enrolled in four-year degree programs, compared to 17 percent of the control group.[27]

ADDITIONAL APPLICATIONS

The following activities represent additional ways to support students through the challenges described in this chapter.

Vision-Reality Exercise

Most people experience tension between a vision of what they want for themselves and the reality of their current situation; this tension can create a positive force to move forward, especially with achieving one's career goals. However, anxiety related to this tension can also cause someone to fall backward by giving up, watering down their vision, or denying reality. In this vision-reality exercise, students are instructed to write notes about their career and related life goals, using tangible, measurable terms so that they can recognize it when it happens. Next, they are asked to honestly state their current reality related to this vision, including things they like, as well as honestly describing what they want to change. After acknowledging this tension, students are then directed to develop and commit to specific steps that they can take toward their vision and to track their results over time.

Bell-Ringing Celebration Ritual

When a student in a current TF cohort (or a recent program graduate) accepts a job offer during the program term, staff hold an impromptu ten-minute celebration ceremony that begins by ringing a bell. Students stand in a group surrounding the newly hired peer, and a program staff member who knows the student asks a series of questions so that the new student can describe the process that led to the job offer and outline their new job, the environment, and the organization. Other students can ask questions as well. The staff member then presents a simply framed quote that captures a strong success quality of this student, reads it aloud, and presents it to the student. This question-and-answer format provides reinforcing instruction on successful job search strategies and soft skills needed for success, imparts information about the job and the work environment, and serves as a powerful reminder that a successful new career launch is within close reach.

Life Philosophy Presentation

The life philosophy presentation is a culminating summary of the inner journey of reflection and growth that students experience during the program. This discussion is designed to vividly demonstrate the relationship between one's philosophy of life and worldview—how we look at ourselves, who we are, and who we can become—especially in response to life's challenges and disruptions. An important perspective to include in the presentation is acceptance of the past as what we needed to experience and learn to bring us to this present moment. Once the burden of regret or bitterness about the past is reduced, students are better able to focus on their future.

One of the program instructors models this process with a candid depiction of the challenges, failures, and disappointments that shook up their own world. Once overcome, these difficult experiences helped to shape their life philosophy, which now has profound effects on their everyday life. The talk is designed to be highly engaging, with visuals such as diagrams and even balloons that get burst as an illustration of how real life's intrusions can burst our illusions of how things ought to be. The students are often shocked to realize that their instructor has gone through deep struggles similar to their own and worked to overcome them. At the close of the talk, students have opportunities to explore how one's philosophy influences behavior, relationships, and decisions. One of the questions that engages everyone is: "How will you take what you have heard today and put it into the grist mill that builds your own life philosophy?" Through this modeling, students have opportunities to explore how their experiences and philosophies influence behavior, relationships, and decisions. The major point is that a philosophy of life can be chosen based on one's unique personal experiences and desires, and can either serve or hinder the decisions one makes and therefore our success in life. The model discussion is full of vivid and motivating stories and examples of people who have experienced limits, faced challenges with integrity, and made choices to break new ground and overcome difficult circumstances. The discussion culminates in a practical list of ways to continue to "grow through life," and how one's philosophies can evolve or deepen through experience.

Graduate Panel Discussion

Many community college programs come to a point in the curriculum at which participants are at risk of falling behind, struggling to master more challenging material, or losing confidence or motivation as the weeks go by. When this point approaches, it is an ideal time to invite a panel of program graduates who have gone on to achieve their goal of launching a new career in this field of study. The best graduates to invite for such a discussion are those who are articulate and down-to-earth, have achieved initial success, have a compelling story of how they got there, and who can relate to the challenges and struggles of the current group. These conversations can be artfully facilitated by an instructor using questions to draw out stories and images of where the graduates were before enrolling, why they chose to enroll, the challenges they encountered and how they addressed them, and where they are now in their lives and careers. Ideal graduate panels include three to six speakers and represent the range of diversity within the group of participants.

Structured Critical Thinking Exercises

Stephen Brookfield, one of the foremost scholars on critical thinking, recommends several considerations for designing structured exercises to help students learn to engage in critical self-reflection.[28]

Students should be placed in small groups with clear ground rules that everyone understands. Learning to think critically is a social process and therefore not easily learned by yourself, but large groups provide neither the psychological safety nor adequate time for each student to engage with the group. The focus and task for everyone involved is to listen carefully to each other, ask questions to help uncover assumptions, and offer alternative perspectives.

The instructor should have modeled the self-reflection process in advance and on multiple occasions, drawing attention to the specifics of what she is doing.

Students should be provided with tangible experiences through which to understand what is going on and practice their critical thinking; some examples Brookfield recommends are case studies, critical incidents, simulations, and scenarios.

Have students begin practicing their critical reflection skills on nonthreatening issues, such as problems or issues related to the academic or professional discipline of the course (for example, chemistry), and only after they have practiced with these skills should they be asked to apply their critical reflection skills to their own thinking.

Peer Mentoring

Some colleges have implemented mentoring systems where incoming students are paired with alumni or students who are nearing graduation. In these mentoring systems, the college establishes communication between the mentor and mentee, provides guidance to the mentor on how to provide appropriate support, and encourages the mentee to take advantage of the relationship by actively communicating with the mentor throughout their time in the program. Some colleges have gone a step further by creating online and face-to-face venues to bring mentors and mentees together.

Sharing Stories

TF uses a modified version of the Toastmasters International public speaking clubs for a special workshop once per week, with speaking topics that often align with the curriculum and workplace cultural expectations and soft skills. For example, students are encouraged to share their experiences in a short-story format on topical themes such as teamwork and overcoming adversity, as well as "educational gem" stories about powerful learning experiences and "icebreaker" stories to introduce themselves. These authentic story-sharing workshops help students realize that others have had similar experiences and create bonds of mutual peer-to-peer support.

FIRST STEPS, OR, "WHAT CAN I DO NOW?"

While one's own experience may differ markedly from those of historically underserved students, self-reflection is nevertheless a valuable way of better understanding this stage of the transformational learning journey. Following are some introductory steps readers can take to prepare themselves to better understand and support this part of the transformation experience for students.

Personal Reflection #1: Disorienting Dilemmas

Think of a time in your life when you experienced a disorienting dilemma that rocked your world and life in a big way. Perhaps it was a big event, such as the birth of a child. Or perhaps a traumatic one, such as the death of a loved one or a major illness. Alternatively, it may be a case where not-so-great life experiences accumulated to a breaking point, where you felt no choice but to initiate a big change in your life. Once you have settled on such an experience, place yourself back in the place and space when you were wrestling with this dilemma and ask yourself these questions:

- What did it feel like when you were experiencing the most acute phase of this moment in your life? What were your thoughts and fears at that moment in time?
- What questions arose for you during this time of uncertainty and searching? In what ways did you question your choices, your viewpoints, and your relationships? If the experience was traumatic, who did you blame for it and why?
- Were there energizing moments during this phase that you experienced? What were these experiences like, and how did these moments contribute to your progress?

- Did you find yourself asking questions about previously held strong beliefs, views, or values? What did it feel like to question such fundamental perspectives?
- Were there people in your life who didn't support the process of change you were going through, who wanted the "old you" back? Who helped you move forward with the changes you needed to make during this tumultuous period, and what did they do that was most helpful?

Personal Reflection #2: Negative Self-Talk Spiral

Think of a domain in your life that you believe that you are just no good at (some possibilities might be art, singing, cooking, household repairs, or sports). For this exercise, it's best to choose something fairly concrete and easy to recall and understand. Once chosen, ask yourself the following questions:

- What do you tell yourself about your inability to do well at this activity? Be specific in quoting your own self-talk!
- How do you feel when you encounter a situation where you are asked to engage in the activity? Are you more likely to initiate action, or to try and avoid it?
- Think about experiences when you encountered difficulty in this activity. What are you feeling and thinking in the moment when you feel yourself struggling? How do these thoughts and feelings affect your ability to concentrate or to problem-solve?
- What goes through your head when you are deciding whether or not to continue engaging in the activity? How long do you allow yourself to struggle? Do you give up? Ask someone else to help or to do it for you?

- How do you feel about talking openly and honestly with people outside of your immediate family and close friends about your struggles in this domain? Do you bring this up to casual acquaintances?
- Raise the stakes about the importance of this domain. How do you think you would feel and respond if others told you that your life's success depended on your ability to perform well in the domain in which you believe you are not very good? This thought exercise may yield insights about the experience of people who know that postsecondary education is the key to their career success, but who quietly harbor doubts and negative self-talk about their ability to be successful college students.

Experimentation

This chapter of the book introduced a number of practices or applications that a community college instructor or advisor may consider to support this leg of the student's transformational learning journey, including:

- Comfort/Discomfort Zone (Inner Pig activity)
- Counseling referrals
- Letting Go balloon exercise
- Quote conversations
- Peer support cohorts
- Holistic, relationship-based advising
- Vision-reality exercise
- Bell-ringing ritual
- Graduate panel discussions
- Structured critical thinking exercises

- Peer mentoring
- Sharing stories

Choose one new activity to experiment with from the above list, from your own experience as a student, or from the self-reflection activity described above. When making your selection, try to fit your choice to your particular students and the kinds of emotional self-assessments and dilemmas they are likely to experience. Choose one method or practice that you find interesting or energizing, that fits your individual role, and for which you have natural opportunities with students, at least some of whom are historically underserved as described in this book. Try it out; document your own observations and your students' responses. Use this introductory practice as a way to more deeply understand students' emotional journeys and how you can support them in this phase.

Interviews

You can also interview historically underserved students whom you know well to learn about their experiences in this part of their journey at college. By interviewing at least three or four students, you will learn more about their experiences and will develop your own insights into how you can support them within your role. Use versions of the questions from the self-reflection questions above as a guide for your student interviews. After conducting the interviews, compare responses from different students to identify common themes, key variances, and ways they have been helped that you and others at the college can adapt to incorporate within your roles.

3

EXPLORING THE PATH FORWARD

"**Y**OU ARE ALREADY DOING THE WORK OF A COLLEGE STUDENT. From this moment on, you're in college," Training Futures program coordinator Susan Craver told trainees one Monday morning a number of years ago. The staff then announced the news that successful completion of coursework at TF would earn its graduates college credits at Northern Virginia Community College (NOVA), thanks to TF's new partnership with NOVA.[1] When asked how they felt after hearing the news about college credit, students responded in unison with the same word, as if this news tapped into a similar script in each life: "Excited!"

Many participants described how this surprise announcement caused them to reassess their perspective about college as an opportunity that they previously did not think was possible. Pedro, for example, had started college but had to quit school to go to work, and he doubted that he would ever be able to restart his higher education. For another participant, the world of US higher education felt like an unknown foreign place: "I wanted to go to college but didn't know how or where to start." As the discussion continued, Amani said, "I always wanted to go to college, but I didn't think I'd be able to afford it." Ghenet echoed Amani's comment, "My friend told me, 'In America, it costs too much to go to college. You'll never afford it.'" Then she turned up the volume on both her smile and her voice, "God bless America!"

One participant talked about how this news could cause a ripple effect with other family members. She planned to go home that day and tell her son, a senior in high school, "Mom is going to college. Why not you?" Another said, "This makes a bright future that's crystal clear. It's a good lesson for my children. Today, I'm going to tell them 'I'm in college!'"

For Connie, the second of nine children in her family, this news held the potential to raise the educational bar for her siblings. "Me and my brother are the only ones who have graduated from high school. I guess we have low standards. No one cared when I quit high school. But I went back and got my diploma. I don't want my brothers and sisters to end up like me: twenty-six years old with few skills." And Connie did not want them to stop with just a high school diploma, either. She says, with an urgent tone in her voice, "You can't even make it with a high school education!"

Before that day, college dreams for these trainees seemed faint and distant, with seemingly tall and imposing barriers surrounding them. Following the surprise announcement, participants found that they were *already* studying—and succeeding—in higher education. Many of the barriers seemed to melt away with Susan's pronouncement: "From this moment on, you're already in college." Because how can barriers prevent you from getting to a place where you already are?

The announcement that participants were already earning NOVA credits triggered in those students a dramatically different view about the accessibility of college and their abilities to succeed in higher education. The carefully facilitated conversation explicitly created a new vision of possibility for students: not only was college no longer out of reach, but they were already performing college coursework and were therefore already college students. This dramatic example shows how others that we trust—in this case an instructor—can provide a compelling vision about ourselves and what is possible.

This chapter describes the need for exploration, for seeing, imagining, and planning possible futures. It focuses on three specific parts of the change process that students are experiencing: the need to explore options, to make a plan, and to acquire the needed knowledge and skills.[2] We offer specific recommendations about how community colleges can—and we believe *should*—approach such tasks as onboarding, advising, and teaching. At the end of the chapter, we provide suggestions for immediate actions readers can take to explore this part of the transformation process.

EXPLORING OPTIONS

One of the key challenges in attempting drastic personal change is that you do not know what you do not know. Therefore, a necessary part of transformation is exploring new possibilities. Mezirow specifically pointed out three areas of exploration necessary. First is exploring new social roles. What are the possibilities for employment, for instance, that are simultaneously realistic but not self-limiting? Relationships are another area. What are the implications of the changes one is experiencing for current relationships? Possibly more important, what are new possibilities for one's current or potential relationships that would align better with the new person one is becoming? Finally, what are the new possibilities for behavior? What are important behavioral tendencies or habits that need to be unlearned, and how should one act in order to succeed in school and at the job one is hoping for?

> I left school after the eleventh grade. Now, I plan to get my GED and graduate from Training Futures at the same time. I really want my GED and college. My dream is to become a counselor, a substance abuse counselor. —*Cassandra, TF alumna*

One tangible area that community college students often need to explore is career options. This can be difficult because they are often unaware of the many possibilities that exist. Like Cassandra, some students enter community college with a definite plan in mind, often because they have some knowledge—and possibly some life experiences—associated with that career. It seems reasonable to assume that most community college students are looking for something better in their lives. As they imagine what their future could hold, they can only really choose from the options that they perceive, and that they perceive to be possible for them. Cassandra may have had some experiences with addiction counselors, saw the good they can do for people, and could envision herself being good in that career while also finding meaning and purpose in it. It is a much bigger challenge for students currently lacking this vision for themselves.

Historically underserved community college students have much lower completion rates, in part because they often do not fully recognize the economic benefits of additional education nor their potential for success in school.[3] The cultural norms, biases, and expectations fostered in students' home environments strongly influence their attitudes toward and choices made in college. For instance, male students and students from high socioeconomic status (SES) backgrounds are more likely than female students and students from low SES backgrounds to pursue more technical areas of study, which are typically more lucrative.[4] Similarly, although African Americans comprise 12 percent of the US population, they only make up 8 percent of general engineering majors, 7 percent of math majors, and 5 percent of computer engineering majors.[5] These three degree programs lead to some of the most lucrative career options; STEM careers can pay up to 50 percent more than those of art, psychology, or social work, which are much more common degree choices for African Americans.[6] We infer from these statistics that social and cultural biases are shaping the choices made by these students. Similar cultural biases may lead many women to conclude that STEM careers are not for them, or men to conclude that nursing is not a suitable career for males. There is nothing wrong with choosing psychology and social work as a degree if that choice is made after careful consideration of one's aptitudes and preferences. But that choice should not be because the students cannot envision themselves as STEM students or, even more important, because the college (unwittingly) steers historically underserved students toward less lucrative degrees through advising, marketing materials, placement-test sorting, and so forth. It is also important to note that careers in psychology and social work often become lucrative only after a graduate degree is earned, and historically underserved students pursue graduate degrees at a much lower rate than their historically served counterparts.

For years, I've had an unstable employment history, not knowing who I am and where I'm going . . . When the employment counselor asked me "what are my goals," I didn't have any, and I sat a long time puzzled . . . I felt I'm running out of time with no goals set and no dreams and no hopes. I just felt my purpose was to raise my children and die. —*Gloria, in a TF graduation speech*

Since students choose their own majors, and sometimes make preliminary choices prior to college enrollment, this challenge is a complex one. For example, the financial aid application (FAFSA) requires students to declare an intended degree or certificate in order to qualify for aid. How do community colleges help eliminate historic and ongoing disparities between career choices and therefore long-term earnings potential between historically served and underserved students? The latter students are the ones most affected by lack of clear vision of possibilities available to them.

When students begin their coursework without a clear vision in mind for what they want to do, it is difficult for them to know what credential to pursue. Should they work toward a credential with immediate application to a career in a trade? Or should they set their sights on transferring to a four-year university because a bachelor's degree might be more beneficial for their career? Their meaning perspectives affect this choice, as they will have deep-seated ideas about their place in society and therefore about the possibilities they perceive as being open to them. Needing to make career choices early so they can make educational decisions, they either choose a program based on what they can relate to (mirroring the employment choices of their parents, for instance) or based on a superficial understanding of what a given career actually entails in terms of preparation or day-to-day practice. Some students forestall this choice and simply begin taking a wide variety of classes that may or may not work together toward a specific degree or certificate. Then, when they finally decide on a program, many find that some of the classes they took cannot be counted toward completing their program. This obviously is a problem for students who have limited time and money to invest in their education.

Historically, some academics have viewed higher education as a time for general exploration. From this perspective, it is good and right for students to take a wide variety of classes in order to gain a wide, balanced general education, as well as to be exposed to diverse academic disciplines. We agree, and at the same time disagree, with this purpose. We agree that higher education should provide an overall learning experience that prepares its graduates to function well in and contribute to democratic society. Martha Nussbaum calls this *cultivating humanity,* describing it as "liberat[ing] the mind from the bondage of habit and custom, producing people who can function with sensitivity and alertness as citizens of the whole world." It should not, she argues, "subordinate the cultivation of the whole person to technical and vocational education."[7] We add Tetyana Kloubert's recommendation that education's purpose is to help people adapt to the world that they live in, but also to develop their "capacity to resist that which is given."[8] This dual purpose of education is especially important for historically underserved students.

However, we disagree with the notion that such an education requires, or is even most effectively accomplished by, students taking entire semester-long courses in multiple, often idiosyncratic subjects in order to gain a well-rounded education. We certainly do not think students should have to invest an entire semester exploring each potential career field. Community colleges should provide a balanced general education that prepares students to fully participate in a democratic society and exposes them to multiple viewpoints and diverse academic disciplines. They should not, however, confine themselves to rigid thinking that would suggest the only way to accomplish those goals is for students to take more semester-long courses than is necessary for their credential. Rather, those higher objectives should be planned for and built into the credential programs.

The approach of taking an excess number of courses for the purpose of exploration might be fine for students for whom the cost and time of education is not a primary concern, but it is not ideal for historically underserved students. This approach is a privilege of the privileged. It is an expensive and time-consuming way of exploring disciplines, and it does not necessarily help with exploring career options because relatively few higher education programs delve into the various careers possible with their courses of study, and even fewer delve into the day-to-day realities of working in those careers.

For historically underserved students, the career choices they perceive themselves to have are primarily those which they have seen filled by people like themselves. Even when exploring more audacious options, a certain career may sound good, but students may not have a realistic concept of what the day-to-day life in that profession would be like, or what additional education may be needed to earn a competitive wage. Students are expected to make decisions about their future, but those decisions can only be made between known options. During this learning process, many students have reported that they begin to see new possibilities at multiple points in time: after gaining new knowledge, feeling a sense of achievement as a learner, or being exposed to career options and professionals that form a new impression. Therefore, their aspirations and goals can be expected to evolve in potentially unexpected ways as they make progress as learners, which can affect decisions about their program of study. And good long-term decisions need to be based on more than limited expectations or even income potential. Students need to be helped to identify those experiences, aptitudes, and preferences that align well with potential majors and careers.[9]

Activities/Supports

One way that many community colleges have chosen to help accelerate the process of exploring options is by deploying new personnel who are often called career navigators. (They may also be called success coaches or career coaches.) Whatever title is used, in most cases these are cross-trained specialists who know about the careers in demand in the local labor market, the academic advising and degrees that lead to those careers, and the support services available at the college and in the community, including scholarships and financial aid. Career navigators are often assigned students, usually from historically underserved groups, when they are just starting their college studies; the navigators get to know the students, develop trust, and act as guides to help them make sense of all of the options for careers and majors that are available to them. Community colleges and their regional partners in Washington state have been among the pioneers for these roles. Several years ago, a published case study at Shoreline Community College, near Seattle, showed that automotive technology students who had an assigned career navigator completed their programs and secured career-track jobs in the industry at rates significantly higher than their peers who had not been assigned a career navigator.[10]

One way of thinking about what needs to happen is through the sociopsychological concept of *possible selves*, the various images that a person can conceive of becoming in the future.[11] These images include what one expects to become, what one hopes to become, and what one is afraid to become.

> These selves provide context for future goals, as well as motivation to achieve them. Since possible selves are rooted in reality (you cannot conceive of a role you do not know exists), helping students develop ambitious but realistic possible selves can help them understand why college is important and become more committed to remaining enrolled.[12]

Students, like all of us, presumably already have a set of possible selves envisioned in the backs of their minds. The challenge for student success arises when the existing possible selves contain only limited possibilities, or when students do not have a realistic view of the steps necessary to achieve them. The objective for community colleges is to ensure that students have the opportunity to develop new possible selves from possibilities they have not considered, as well as to develop realistic plans for achieving those visions of themselves. A particularly powerful and necessary part of this process is to clarify the role that a college education plays in achieving these goals. Possible selves "take students' idealized visions of the future and turn them into concrete, actionable goals that require a college degree."[13] Having a compelling justification for a college degree helps students persevere through the inevitable challenges of their higher education experience.

Advising   Part of any holistic approach to this work has to include advising, and we recognize that many colleges are already evaluating their advising practices to promote student success. For our purposes here, we provide a few specific suggestions for helping students explore options for new roles, relationships, and actions.

During or prior to the onboarding process of new students, there should be an emphasis on up-front advising focused on helping students explore potential program and career options. Most community colleges already attempt to do this, and we acknowledge the difficulties involved. Foremost among these challenges is the high student case load that most advisors have. Recognizing that advisors have a finite amount of time, care should be taken to separate the functions of information-providing from one-on-one consultation. Advisors need time to give individual attention to students; it is not efficient for advisors to spend their time imparting information that could be conveyed otherwise through printed materials and online resources. Melinda Karp recommends, for instance, that colleges create video vignettes, accessible online, that demonstrate students pursuing different career paths, along with their decision-making processes and their plans for achieving their goals.[14] Videos like this not only convey information about possible credentials and careers, they help students envision themselves in those credential programs and careers, exploring possible selves while also learning about the college's role in making those possibilities a reality.[15]

An increasingly common practice is to require all students to take a course that introduces them to life in college, provides training in study skills and how to be a successful college student, and helps them explore possible careers that align with their unique experiences, aptitudes, and preferences. To the extent possible, colleges should work with local industries to devise ways to convey to students what the day-to-day experience is like for various careers. We recommend approaching this course as a prolonged series of advising activities, where advising is treated as a developmental mentoring activity.[16] So rather than having one instructor, the course utilizes multiple advisors, faculty, and other key stakeholders who participate in ongoing and meaningful ways with students. This course can include a variety of self-assessments designed to help students explore potential career possibilities and how they match with them. According to the student needs described by Thomas Bailey, Timothy Leinbach, and Davis Jenkins, the focus of such a course could be fourfold: to help students 1) explore a variety of viable careers and their respective credential programs; 2) understand the long-term implications of those choices; 3) make concrete plans to obtain these goals; and 4) develop the skills to accomplish them effectively.[17]

It is especially important for colleges to evaluate their advising practices, and especially their printed and online images, to ensure that historically underserved students are not unintentionally pointed toward lower-paying career fields. In fact, special attention should be given to helping these students become aware of more lucrative careers and see themselves as viable candidates for those careers. Students need to understand the relative salaries of various career choices. High aspirations are beneficial to community college student success.[18] Colleges should therefore push students to consider and commit to ambitious credential and career options that align well with their goals and potentialities.

As a final caveat, we do not advocate promoting unrealistic credential expectations. There is a balance to be found in exploring possibilities that are simultaneously realistic but not self-limiting. It is important that artificial limits are not placed on students based on race, gender, or social class. However, if students are unlikely to be accepted into a limited-access program (such as nursing) because of past grades or other admissions criteria, then it is only fair to encourage them to also consider more viable options.[19] These other options are not necessarily less lucrative. Nursing, for instance, is usually a limited-access program because the costs to provide such an education are much higher than for other careers; it is not because nursing is more lucrative than those careers.

Students greatly value their community college advisors, as the following quotes from TF students who had ongoing relationships with an assigned college advisor or success coach illustrates.

> Anytime I have a question, I can send [my assigned advisor] an email. It was a good feeling for me because I was thinking, "Okay, somebody is going to be there for me."

> Our lives as adults are complex. That person [the advisor] knows already what you're doing, what's your experience, what's your background.

> Sometimes [my assigned advisor] gives me the strength, support, and energy when we're this close to giving up.

> I remember mentioning to [my assigned advisor] what if I take religion, and sociology and psychology? And she's like, "No, let's finish your associate's degree. You need to complete that. That's your goal."

Internships Similarly, students value internships and other work-based learning experiences that community colleges provide for them. These new learning and life experiences often reveal new options that may not have been visible before. When TF participants return from two-week internships, instructors facilitate a conversation about their experiences and what they learned about themselves and their next career steps from these experiences. One cohort's discussion included the following observations.

I had forgotten how much I missed being in an office. I had a myth of government workers just trying to look busy, but they were diligent and did fantastic customer service. —*Karen, returning from an internship with a local government agency*

This was my first time in a business office environment. I saw how people handled themselves. I'm open now for anything. —*Elizabeth*

This is the place I want to be. I really listened to the sales manager. He's my role model. It's my dream job. I can see myself there now, even though I have further to climb. —*Joseph, returning from an internship in the sales department of a hotel*

Advising and work-based learning experiences can open up new possibilities, or they can help a participant rule out a specific type of role or work environment. As Joseph observed, each learning and work experience can open up a new vista of possibilities that were unimagined previously because they were unknown.

Student Testimony

After the first couple of weeks I can see how the way I see life is different and how I have to set up goals and be determined on what I want. —*Cynthia, a TF graduate*

I started school [at NOVA before Training Futures], but my ex [husband] said, "No more, you're not able to study." So, it was really hard because I didn't know about the process, like you have to withdraw by a certain date, and they have deadlines. So, I had Ws in many of my records, because I didn't know that I wasn't supposed to just leave the class . . . Training Futures gave me a counselor . . . She helped me with a petition we needed to do to appeal for the dean to basically forgive me because I didn't complete those classes. It was something that I didn't know, but the dean approved . . . [Now] I have the support, and I have the guidance, something that I didn't have before. —*Rosina, a TF graduate who worked closely with a navigator at NOVA*

Breaking free of one's familiar routines to create new plans aiming for an unfamiliar future life and career can be a long journey, fraught with many challenges, as well as stops and starts along the way. In recounting her difficult journey as her TF cohort's graduation speaker, Janice told the audience that she decided "as a child that I would be different . . . so I worked hard trying to avoid their mistakes. . . . But there was no structure or guidance in my home throughout my childhood and teen years. It was all very negative. . . . One time during a fight between my brother's father and my mother's boyfriend, I was caught in the crossfire and shot in both legs. By age fifteen, I was pregnant and left my mother's home."

Janice's plans for a different life were repeatedly derailed by self-destructive behaviors that resembled patterns she experienced growing up, including teenage rebellion and later by quitting a good job and becoming increasingly dependent upon public assistance. She reflected on these years of struggle: "I didn't realize that I was doing the same thing, only differently." Following the premature birth of her second daughter, Janice regained her resolve to change. "She only weighed two pounds at birth . . . My daughter held onto life by a thread and somehow survived beyond all the odds against her . . . I knew that if I could make it through this with her, I could make it through any ordeal."

Janice went on to describe her discoveries at TF that helped inform her plans for a new career. "I went from zero to forty words per minute in typing, and I love filing, a job most people love to hate." On her internship, she "answered busy phones, quickly learned my way around their database, and trained a coworker in Excel . . . This reinforced in me that I could do it!" Janice described her plan to continue exploring her career options through temporary positions before finding a permanent job.

Three months after completing the program, Janice returned to TF to celebrate her new permanent job and shared her story with the next cohort of participants. She told them: "One year ago this month, I walked into Fairfax County's [social services] building to meet with them about the VIEW program.[20] As I walked into that building, I thought I was a nobody. And now, I work there!" Her plans have expanded far beyond what she previously thought was possible. She concluded her remarks by saying: "Ordinary is no longer enough. I'm going for extraordinary!"

Like Janice, many TF participants have described a similar evolving pattern to their plans. Until they begin mastering new skills, gaining confidence, and learning more about potential opportunities to apply their skills in new careers, it is difficult for many participants to even envision what more might be possible. Setbacks encountered along the way are common and can pause, stop, or redirect plans, especially if one reflects on what these experiences have to tell us, as Janice did after the birth of her second daughter.

MAKING A PLAN

Navigating a river on a dark night is an arduous, if not terrifying, task—one best left to seasoned professionals—and one that

Judith Scott-Clayton claims is an apt metaphor for what community college students have to do in order to complete a degree.[21] Specifically, she refers to the myriad tasks and obstacles from initial entry into college all the way through completion that students are usually expected to do without any clear and obvious structure. "Without signposts, without a guide, without a visible shoreline to follow, many students make false starts, take wrong turns, and hit unexpected obstacles, while others simply 'kill the boat' trying to figure out where they are."[22]

At some point, there are concrete steps that need to be taken if someone is going to make deep and lasting changes, and therefore a plan needs to be created for what those steps should be. For historically underserved community college students, the mere fact that they are attending college is an indication that they have thought about and possibly created some type of plan. The problem is that many students do not know enough about the college's system, or about higher education's practices and norms in general, to be able to craft the specifics of a plan that will lead to the completion of the credential—and therefore to their hoped-for career outcomes. And the historical structure of community colleges have caused many students to flounder, waste credit hours, and ultimately leave school without completing a credential. Knowing this, it is incumbent on the community college to plan for, prepare, and help students make a realistic and detailed plan to accomplish their educational goals. In short, colleges need to create the educational plan or roadmap for students who want to achieve specific targeted career pathways that are in high demand in their service regions.

Guided Pathways

Colleges are and will always be in a better position than individuals to understand the changing labor market and employer needs in their regions, and to know what skills and credentials are needed to qualify for employment in these in-demand fields. Colleges need to build and rely on their own institutional expertise to make career pathway plans for students to follow, instead of leaving students on their own to guess at what potential in-demand careers might be and figure out how to navigate the college's labyrinthine system.

Based on the observation of the myriad tasks and obstacles confronted by community college students that inhibit their progress toward credential completion, Scott-Clayton argues for stronger and more rigid frameworks to help students complete their degrees efficiently and at higher rates. She calls her argument the *structure hypothesis*, which claims that "students will be more likely to persist and succeed in programs that are tightly and consciously structured, with relatively little room for individuals to deviate on a whim—or even unintentionally—from paths toward completion, and with limited bureaucratic obstacles for students to circumnavigate."[23] The lineage of her arguments can be traced from Vincent Tinto's work on student persistence in 1993 to James Rosenbaum, Regina Deil-Amen, and Ann Person's work in 2006.[24] This line of reasoning has become more pronounced and vocal, and is currently one of the main rallying cries of community college reform, as can be seen in efforts such as Completion by Design, as well as in repeated calls for the implementation of guided pathways.[25]

Why is more structure so important? For one, less structure inevitably leads to greater complexity for students. True, with a cafeteria-style offering of courses and programs, students have all the freedom they could desire to design a customized educational experience, but only if they possess the cultural understandings needed to benefit from that freedom. More important, most community college students are not primarily seeking a customized educational experience. They are choosing to enroll in college because they want a credential that will lead to a life-sustaining job and career. Structure is important because those students from historically underserved backgrounds are less likely to have the cultural knowledge or social networks they can rely upon to provide guidance in navigating the college's array of programs and courses.[26] Not having access to cultural knowledge or personal social networks, these students rely more heavily on the institution to provide such guidance. And, of course, providing the individualized guidance necessary to help students navigate a complex, unstructured system is prohibitively expensive for most community colleges. This guidance is much less necessary when colleges take a proactive approach to designing their curricular offerings based on desired labor market outcomes and their respective credentials, and having systematic, structured course sequences that lead to those credentials. These reasons are why we are so supportive of the guided pathways movement.[27]

Many college advisors (as well as career navigators at colleges that have deployed these cross-trained specialists) use career pathway planning to assist students in exploring and determining their career goals and in formulating an educational plan that goes beyond the initial entry-level professional job to include further career advancement opportunities. Students often begin with a guided exploration of online information about employer demand for various professions, along with descriptions of various careers. Most student service departments also have career aptitude or interest tests available that can assist students in narrowing down fields that match their interests. Once students identify a professional field of interest, advisors can use career pathway maps to determine education and credential requirements for entry-level and next-level occupations within the profession. As described in this chapter, career pathway plans may include specific semester-by-semester course sequence recommendations so that students have a clear road map for their community college career education.

ACQUIRING NEEDED KNOWLEDGE AND SKILLS

In the first week of training, TF students write themselves a letter, to be opened and read later in the program as they prepare to embark on internships. Tracy's letter included, "I am attending (school) to be a winning success. I have a lot of street knowledge and now I will have book knowledge too."

A cursory glance may suggest that this book's message downplays the importance of the knowledge and skills found on course syllabi. That is not true at all. In order for people to accomplish the plan they create for their future, they must acquire the knowledge and skills necessary to enact it. Community colleges have traditionally focused programs of study on the technical knowledge and skills required for specific occupations, and most have developed instructional systems to transmit and assess this knowledge. However, we feel that other key aspects of curricular choices, design, and delivery should be done differently. And if our recommendations are followed, we believe all students, especially historically underserved students, will be much better prepared to complete their credentials and obtain and excel at their career goals.

> Training Futures taught me lessons for living, not just practical office skills. It emphasized life skills like time management, interpersonal communication, and overcoming obstacles to achieve goals.

Training Futures for me was strict but supportive. Before Training Futures, I was on food stamps, housing aid, and in a bad relationship. Now I have a new car, a new job I love, and positive people in my life. —*Juanita*

One Human Resources director who recruited many staff from TF said this about candidates from the program: "The graduates really care about the quality of their work. They learned to pay attention to details and so they make fewer mistakes. They bring a positive, can-do approach to their jobs that helps lift their work teams." A company executive wrote this about an intern that she hired: "She easily earned the trust of office mates immediately . . . She demonstrated a sincere loyalty and commitment to her work and the people around her. Her powerful combination of software application skills and committed loyalty make her an excellent addition to any team."

This section illustrates some types of knowledge, skills, and attitudes that are necessary for success in school and the labor market but that are often omitted from community college curricula. It then discusses the ways that classroom and curricular design impact the learning process and proposes radical changes to how community colleges think about their learning spaces and practices.

What Should Be Taught, Part One: Curricular Design and Threshold Concepts

The best way to illustrate the point we want to make about curricular design is perhaps to tell a personal story. Coauthor Chad Hoggan pursued an undergraduate degree in business management, and he tells this story about his required courses in accounting: My academic identity was as a math person. I felt that I could not write papers very well, but math always came really easily for me. Looking forward to my introductory accounting class and assuming it would be easy, I was shocked when I performed poorly on my first two quizzes. I had studied for them but simply did not seem to *get it*. So, I made the decision one Saturday to study for as long as it took until I understood my accounting work. A few hours into this study session, something clicked. I realized that accounting—at a practical level—is all about balance. On an income statement, if a particular amount of money comes in as income at the top of the statement, it has to go out, usually as an increase in profits, in the bottom half of the statement in order for things to balance. Similarly, if there is an increase in assets in the balance sheet, there must be a corresponding decrease in another asset or an increase in the liabilities sections of the statement. For instance, if a customer pays an invoice and therefore a sum of money increases the checking account (an asset), the accounts receivable (another asset: the money customers owe you) should decrease by the same amount, because the customer who just paid no longer owes you that money. So in this case, one asset (cash) was increased and therefore another asset (money that people owe you) had to decrease. Once this way of thinking about recording money occurred to me, everything else in the course clicked. The class went from being impossible to easy.

Here is the problem: neither the instructor nor the textbook ever mentioned this way of thinking. For me, it was by far the most important thing I learned, because it affected everything else, but it was not intuitive. Because of this epiphany, the discipline and practices of accounting made so much more sense. Thus, what ended up being the most important learning was neither articulated nor planned for; it was either learned or *not* learned via immersion in lectures and homework assignments.

Relatively recently, higher education scholars have begun to talk about learning experiences like the one I had. They call the phenomenon *threshold concepts*.[28] In essence, this idea proposes that every field or discipline has one or more key understandings that act as a gatekeeper for newcomers. (Hence, "threshold" concepts; they determine whether newcomers are able to cross the threshold into the field.) Whether newcomers ever understand the key knowledge and skills of the discipline is predicated on their ability to learn these core understandings. And conversely, threshold concepts form a barrier to newcomers unless and until they are learned.

Knowing this, it is incumbent on faculty, and preferably whole programs, to invest the time necessary to figure out these tacit, behind-the-scenes ways of thinking, understanding, and being that are critical in order for their students to succeed as newcomers in their discipline. A key challenge to identifying threshold concepts is that sometimes they are applicable to the entire discipline (like the accounting example), but other times they may be unique to each niche within a discipline. Therefore, some understanding of the characteristics of threshold concepts might be helpful for faculty to try to figure out what these gatekeeper learnings are for their disciplines. According to Jan Meyer and Ray Land, threshold concepts are:

Transformative: Threshold concepts significantly change the learner's perception of and participation with a subject.

Irreversible: Threshold concepts are not likely to be forgotten or unlearned.

Integrative: Threshold concepts change the student's entire conception of the subject. Previously hidden interrelations between topics in the discipline become more visible and better understood.

Troublesome: Threshold concepts are often difficult for new-comers to grasp. Faculty have historically not focused on them and made them visible, and the concepts can seem counterintuitive, alien, or incoherent to people not fully acclimated to a discipline and its unique ways of thinking, understanding, and being. [29]

Faculty trying to identify threshold concepts in their own disci-plines may benefit from asking themselves the following questions:

- Where do fundamental shifts in understanding come from?
- What do students in introductory classes seem to especially struggle to understand?
- For these topics, what are underlying, tacit, or otherwise hidden understandings that help make learning them easier?

A key implication here is that instruction time does not have to be—and should not be—allocated equally across all topics. Instead, curricular design needs to shift so that threshold con-cepts are not only explicitly included, but focused on. Sufficient time should be devoted to these key understandings before mov-ing on to other areas. Threshold concepts need to be articulated, taught thoughtfully, and covered as early in a course and program as appropriate, given necessary prerequisite knowledge. Time in-vested early in the learning process on threshold concepts will be made up for throughout the term as other, often difficult con-cepts are grasped more easily and quickly by students who are equipped with the concepts and skills necessary to truly under-stand all of the topics in the course. This approach to teaching is helpful for all students, but it is especially necessary for historically underserved students who often have not had access to mentors and role models in their respective disciplines from whom they might pick up these key understandings through conversations and other forms of social interaction.

What Should Be Taught, Part Two: The Softer Side

Numerous surveys of employers in many business sectors have pointed to gaps in what are often described as "soft skills," especially among newly trained or newly hired workers. Examples of employer-valued soft skills often include teamwork, attendance, time management, problem-solving, communication, and accepting criticism. Even a cursory review of these abilities suggests that they are often attitudes or habits with deep roots in experiences, relationships, and cultures. Developing soft skills is not something that can be accomplished by reading about them. These qualities need to be integrated with the technical knowledge and hands-on performance that typically comprise the curriculum focus in a college program of study.

A review of the self-evaluation reports completed by participants following one TF cohort highlights some of the soft skills that participants can develop when the curriculum offers more of a holistic immersion in a simulated office environment. When asked to compare the "old me" to the "new me" on their evaluations, participants often mentioned a range of personal qualities that suggest deeper changes that translate into the kinds of skills that employers prize.

For example, Agnes wrote that the old me would "continue to make excuses, have no time management and didn't look at myself as a leader." Her new me has "time management, [is] a potential leader, more dedicated, and no more excuses!"

Ashley observed that the old me was "dressing down/casual, not thinking positively and with bad habits." Her new me is "dressing up, positively thinking and hoping for the best, and knocking out bad habits."

Gabu commented that the old me "was in an argument when I found something different from my opinion." With his new me, "I can easily accept any kinds of tasks even if it is hard for me, and I don't want to argue."

Self-reflective comments such as these provide glimpses of the changes and resulting attitudes and qualities that complement the knowledge learned in the formal content curriculum. They also point to an important dimension of transformational learning that is often overlooked: in order to make deep changes, students often have to "unlearn" previous ways of thinking and long-term habits, a process that is more difficult than merely acquiring new knowledge. Another student in this cohort, Melody, wrote this advice to future students on her evaluation form:

> Don't be the enemy that holds you back. If you came to [school], you're already on your way to self-improvement. This is more than just a re-training program; it's about the experience and most importantly, personal growth . . . Lastly, don't be too hard on yourself. Nobody's perfect and in time, you too will get there. Just believe.

In short, we are advocating that program faculty take a serious look at the soft skills that their students and graduates need in order to be successful in the careers of their discipline, and to explicitly incorporate the development of those soft skills into the curriculum. We are not the first voices to say this. In one recent report, Brent Orrell[30] demonstrated, based on labor market data and employer feedback, that even important STEM-related skills are not enough to improve labor market outcomes; soft skills such as listening, problem-solving, teamwork, integrity, and dependability are increasingly needed and valued in middle-skill jobs.

Often, these skills can be explicitly embedded within many work-based learning instructional methods, such as learning about teamwork in project-based learning group assignments, learning the importance of showing up on time with points deducted for unexcused late arrivals to class, learning about workplace cultures from guest speakers from industry or site visits with employers, or learning how to accept and respond to feedback and criticism from individualized midterm performance reviews by the instructor.

How Teaching Should Occur: Context and Learning Transfer

It is impossible to separate *what* is learned from *how* it is learned. Misunderstanding this maxim leads to situations where students feel that what they are learning is irrelevant, that learning is intimidating, and that classroom learning does not transfer or relate to actual practice. By deciding what to teach and how to teach it based on historical precedent, or by falling back on "that's just the way things are done here at this college or in my discipline," we as educators do students a great disservice. Many of the practices and norms of higher education are simply not the same as the practices and norms of practitioners, and they do not make sense in actual practice. Since our students presumably want to become practitioners, that is a problem.

One of the most important insights into human learning came about from a study conducted back in the mid-1980s. Jean Lave was interested in how adults did relatively complex problems in the context of their daily lives and how that might compare to the math they learned in school. She found that her participants were able to perform relatively complicated computations when doing price comparison shopping—and being accurate an astounding 98 percent of the time. They performed these computations using various elements of the setting (the store and its contents) and the process of shopping.[31]

> One shopper accurately determined an incorrectly marked product by comparing its weight-price relation with other similarly weighted products rather than computing the actual per pound cost and then checking it with that printed on the package (which is the solution that school-taught mathematics would have preferred). That is, the elements of the setting—the actual grocery items, not computational procedures—were used to check discrepancies.[32]

However, when adults in a classroom setting were administered a paper-and-pencil test *for the same types of computations* (but insisting on the use of ratios for making price comparisons rather than creatively using elements of the store context), the adults' error-free math solutions dropped from 98 percent in the store to 59 percent in the classroom. Lave's primary conclusion was that you cannot separate thinking from the practice in which it happens; thinking always occurs in physical and social contexts and is structured by situationally provided tools. In fact, the use of tools that are appropriate to the actual practice of a discipline is an essential part of a good and practical education. This notion of the importance of practice, context, and tools on thinking and learning is often referred to as *situated cognition.* John Seely Brown, Allan Collins, and Paul Duguid offer an excellent description of the necessity of learning school content using authentic problems and tools, as well as the damage that occurs from most current educational approaches.

> People who use tools actively rather than just acquire them, by contrast, build an increasingly rich implicit understanding of the world in which they use the tools and of the tools themselves. The understanding, both of the world and of the tool, continually changes as a result of their interaction. Learning and acting are interestingly indistinct, learning being a continuous, lifelong process resulting from acting in situations.
>
> Too often the practices of contemporary schooling deny students the chance to engage the relevant domain culture, because that culture is not in evidence. Although students are shown the tools of many academic cultures in the course of a school career, the pervasive cultures that they observe, in which they participate, and which some enter quite effectively are the cultures of school life itself. These cultures can be unintentionally antithetical to useful domain learning. . . . Thus, students may pass exams (a distinctive part of school cultures) but still not be able to use a domain's conceptual tools in authentic practice. . . .
>
> In order to learn these subjects (and not just to learn about them) students need much more than abstract concepts and self-contained examples. They need to be exposed to the use of a domain's conceptual tools in authentic activity—to teachers acting as practitioners and using these tools in wrestling with problems of the world. Such activity can tease out the way a mathematician or historian looks at the world and solves emergent problems. The process may appear informal, but it is nonetheless full-blooded, authentic activity that can be deeply informative—in a way that textbook examples and declarative explanations are not. . . .

Math word problems, for instance, are generally encoded in a syntax and diction that is common only to other math problems. . . . By participating in such ersatz activities students are likely to misconceive entirely what practitioners actually do. As a result, students can easily be introduced to a formalistic, intimidating view of math that encourages a culture of math phobia rather than one of authentic math activity.[33]

We would like to emphasize the main point being made here and be explicit about its implications for community colleges. There are norms and practices that function as tools that shape the thinking and learning in higher education and yet are detrimental to student learning, to learning transfer, and to the labor market outcomes of graduates. Traditional knowledge-based tests, for instance, are one such tool. Such tests are ubiquitous in higher education, and the ability to perform well on tests is a paramount skill to be successful in school. Therefore, learning to take tests is a skill that is unique to and only provides benefits in school cultures, and as such is constantly promoted and reinforced. It has little value to the learner beyond the school context. So students learn the use of a tool that they will not use again after their education. Worse, the thinking and problem-solving patterns developed through the use of that tool, and thereby shaped by that tool, are different from the thinking and problem-solving patterns that graduates will need to use when their jobs require them to engage in authentic tasks.

Students, therefore, graduate with a useless skill at the expense of developing skills that *would* be useful in the contexts for which the education was supposed to be preparing them. To this point we argue that programs should take a critical look at what their students need to be able to do with the education they are being given, and at the tools (conceptual and physical) used in the actual practice of their discipline, and then design the learning environment and pedagogical processes such that students gain experience and skills in the use of discipline-specific tools as applied to authentic tasks for that discipline. Students should develop those skills rather than school-centric skills such as test-taking abilities.

As a case in point, TF does not have their students sit at desks in a classroom. Instead, they designed their learning spaces to resemble an office environment. They also design their practices to mirror the norms that their students will likely experience in their future workplaces. One such practice, for instance, is that students clock in and out, using time cards. Instead of receiving a deduction in their grade for arriving late or missing class, they receive verbal or written warnings based on system similar to the workplaces in which students are likely to work. If they are late or miss a class, they are asked to follow up with an email to their program supervisor affirming their commitment to punctuality and attendance, and they can be terminated from the program if attendance problems continue. To illustrate how important workplace cultural immersion was for TF, the program management team turned down an offer by NOVA for free space on one of its campuses so that it could remain located within a business district, surrounded by business professionals and the cultural artifacts of the business world, rather than being on a college campus apart from that immersive experience. While relocating most college programs elsewhere is not feasible, systematic use of such immersion practices within a curriculum or program of study can help students learn and become comfortable with the day-to-day lived reality of the career for which they are preparing. This is such an insightful approach to teaching because it aligns the learning context with the working context in which that learning will eventually need to be applied.

ADDITIONAL APPLICATIONS

Employer Engagement

College program leaders can expose students to a variety of professional settings with various forms of employer engagement activities, which help students form more concrete and realistic images of the professional environment for which they are training. Many programs, including TF, host employer representatives as guest speakers, so that students can learn directly from them about job expectations, workplace environments, and the application process. Programs can coordinate site visits for students with nearby employers, which makes the exposure even more vivid. Even better, programs can arrange job shadowing, in which a student is assigned to observe a specific professional for a specific period of time, often for one day, including opportunities to talk with this mentor about the job.

Collaborating with Stakeholders

Community colleges can work with local K–12 systems to codesign career exploration programs so that students can begin exploring career possibilities as early as middle school. The intent here is not to try to force students to make career decisions before they are fifteen years old, but rather to help them gain an understanding of the vast range of possibilities and develop a sense of efficacy in choosing a career. It is especially important to have these career exploration programs available for students from historically underserved backgrounds and to ensure that the images used in those programs include professionals with whom the students can relate; in order for students to develop a possible self that includes being a professional in a lucrative career, it helps to see people who look like them already in those careers.

Community colleges can also work with local high schools to expose students to the specific program areas offered at the college, as well as to the careers that are possible from each program. The idea is to help students develop "idealized visions of the future and turn them into concrete, actionable goals that require a college degree."[34] Community colleges' marketing efforts should help students imagine themselves in various professional roles by ensuring that images in their publications or on their websites represent the full range of student demographics. Also, graduating students and alumni can be engaged in marketing efforts to help current students envision their own success by seeing how their peers were able to succeed.

Performance Review Meetings

At TF, students experience three performance review meetings with an assigned advisor, who collects and relays feedback from other staff and self-evaluation from the student in a process that simulates workplace performance reviews. At these meetings with a trusted faculty advisor, the student and advisor honestly discuss successes to build upon, as well as challenges and mistakes to address, with specific corrective actions to take. They also discuss the student's professional goals, how their current studies support their goals, and other actions to undertake in students' ongoing professional development.

Getting and Keeping a Job Curriculum

The Getting and Keeping a Job (GKJ) workshops are designed to erase the mystique and past failure associated with not knowing the hidden rules of job searching with concrete, methodological training and an extensive manual for self-study and reference. Upon completing GKJ activities, students understand what they need to do in order to get a job offer, and how to successfully transition into the world of work in their field. *Aha!* moments during GKJ workshops are common, with students saying things like, "Now I understand why I didn't get that job!" Guest presenters who work in the training program's targeted occupations, such as hiring managers and recruiters, share behind-the-scenes insights, insider tips, and personal experiences. Each workshop is designed to take apart a specific job search skill, explain it in simple terms with practical guidelines, and have the student immediately design and practice an individual response using step-by-step tools or worksheets. For example: What is an interviewer really looking for when saying, "Tell me about yourself," and other common interview questions. The students prepare responses and present them in a small group for practice and feedback. Finally, the entire group convenes to discuss what was learned. The key is imparting ownership and confidence through mastery. The culmination of this activity comes at the end of the two-week curriculum, when guests from local businesses conduct practice interviews. Program-specific job fairs immediately follow this activity, which are powerful because students experience their employable "new me" through the eyes of actual employers who have come exclusively to conduct screening interviews just for them.

As the GKJ time frame progresses, students get job offers and begin leaving the program to start work, while others continue their job search. For those whose job search continues, daily job club meetings are designed to prevent isolation and sustain the individual student in a supportive community of fellow job seekers. In these meetings, handouts on further aspects of the job search process are discussed to continue building and refreshing job search skills, and job club members report on results and questions from calls, interviews, and networking. Breakthroughs are celebrated, and struggles are shared.

The overall purpose of the GKJ curriculum is to build a foundation of success before sending students out on their own. Nerves and anxieties are handled in a supportive, "this is your process" understanding that includes repeated, built-in, individualized feedback within a fast-paced curriculum flow that does not allow time for old fears to interfere. Each week during the GKJ curriculum, celebrations are held to highlight the often surprising volume of skills and understandings that have been accomplished in such a short time.

Immersion in a Social Context

Another unique aspect of educational contexts is the traditional classroom environment, with seats that face the front of the room and an instructor playing the part of "sage on the stage." The immersive learning methods described earlier in this chapter involve significant changes and planning. However, even something as simple as rearranging seats in a classroom can have a big impact on the way students engage in a class, how they interpret themselves in relation to the course material, and how they see themselves as learners and consumers of knowledge. Something as simple as arranging seating so that there are multiple small groupings of students sitting around tables will orient learners toward each other and encourage discussion among them. Similarly, having seats arranged in a large circle promotes large group discussion and sends the message that important knowledge resides, at least in part, among everyone in the class. Many more classroom designs are possible, including roundtable meeting arrangements like those common in many office environments, and they should be considered in terms of the implicit messages they send and their effect on student learning.

To take this idea a step further, the classroom environment itself could and should be evaluated. One of the unique aspects of TF is a focus on providing an education that allows graduates to seamlessly step into a job. Because their goal is to help low-income adults secure life-sustaining jobs in office careers, their learning spaces replicate an office environment rather than a typical classroom. As mentioned earlier, students clock in and clock out. If they are late or miss a day of training, they are given verbal and/or written warnings according to a strict schedule. Everyone is expected to wear office-appropriate attire and speak in office-appropriate language. They even participate in networking events with other students, faculty, alumni, and community partners so they can learn and get comfortable with that aspect of professional life. (More details about TF and its structure can be found in the appendix.)

The recommendation we are making is that each program should look carefully at the understandings, customs, and norms that comprise the tools of practice of their discipline—and find ways to incorporate those tools and authentic activities into a purposeful pedagogical system that helps students become adept as practitioners of the discipline rather than adept at the norms of higher education.

Work-Based Simulations and Projects

At TF, most of the learning activities and assignments are designed to closely simulate practices at work. For example, in business writing, students practice writing emails and are assigned email mentors with whom to practice professional correspondence. In customer service, students rotate through short shifts answering the main TF phones under the supervision of the office manager. Students also practice organizing files using a file management simulation, develop and present PowerPoint presentations, and develop and perform spreadsheet calculations for expense tracking simulations. Each of these dozens of simulated or actual work-based learning assignments helps to sharpen their skills and ensure that they can perform them within a typical workplace context. In contrast, a more typical college sequence might involve traditional classroom learning followed sometime later by a clinical placement or internship.

An Immersive Environment

One's surroundings can subtly influence perception, thinking, and behavior in many ways. College faculty and program administrators can organize a learning environment in which students are surrounded by visual cues that they are preparing for the workplace. Many programs strive to have industry-standard equipment, software, and materials for students to use in completing applied learning assignments. However, there are many opportunities to go further in creating an immersive environment that reinforces the learning needed for the workplace. For example, hung on the walls at TF are posters with inspirational images and quotes that reinforce the soft skills needed for the workplace. There are also posters with photos of program graduates, along with information about their career successes and quotes from these former students about their learning experiences at TF. There's a break room, common to many workplaces, with a table where peers can gather over coffee or lunch, along with signs about the shared responsibilities to keep the room clean and contribute to shared supplies like coffee.

FIRST STEPS, OR, "WHAT CAN I DO NOW?"

While one's own experience may differ markedly from those of historically underserved students, self-reflection is nevertheless a valuable way of better understanding this stage of the transformational learning journey. Following are some introductory steps readers can take to prepare themselves to better understand and support this part of the transformation experience for students.

Personal Reflection

Think about a time when you needed to change direction in a significant way in your life. Perhaps it was traveling away from home and your parents' constraints for the first time, maybe even an initial experience at college. Or perhaps it involved a major career switch from one field to a very different field that required additional study or preparation. Whatever life change you choose, try to picture yourself in that time and place, and explore a few reflection questions:

- What was your goal, and what process or experiences led you to the point where you decided on your new direction? Who helped you in this process, and what specifically did this person do that was most helpful for you?
- What steps did you have to take to get from where you were to where you wanted to be? How did you know or learn the steps needed to get there? What hurdles did you face along the way, and how did you work to get past these hurdles? Who helped you and how?
- Looking back on the early days of your new role/place/job, what did you already know or expect, and how did you learn about them? What did you have to learn the hard way

through painful mistakes, and what did you wish you knew beforehand? What could someone else, such as a mentor or teacher, have warned you about or taught you?

- Thinking about your reflections on each of these questions, what can you do in your role to help support students going through this stage of exploring options?

Experimentation

In this chapter, we have outlined a number of methods and applications that college faculty and advisors can use to support students in exploring paths forward. These include:

- Holistic advising/career navigators
- Guided pathways
- College success skills courses
- Teaching threshold concepts
- Embedding soft skills training within the curriculum
- Contextualized math (or other topics)
- Employer engagement in the curriculum
- Collaborations with K–12 stakeholders
- Performance review meetings with students
- Getting and Keeping a Job curriculum
- Rearranging the learning space/immersive environment
- Work-based learning/simulations/project-based learning

Think about one of these methods, either from your self-reflection exercise or the list above, that would support your students in exploring their roles in some way. Choose one that you think could make a difference in your students' ability to make a plan. Try it out, observe your students' responses to the activity or method, and ask them whether or how it helped them.

Interviews

Select several students you know who come from a background in which they may have had little exposure to a field of study that they later undertook. Ask them about their experiences in making a plan. You can use the same questions listed above in the self-reflection activity. Compare what you learned about their experiences to yours, and also compare the experiences among different students you interviewed. What stood out for you from these conversations? What have you learned from each of these explorations that can inform your own plan about supporting students in these phases of their journey?

4

REINTEGRATION

D EBORAH, THE LAST STUDENT SPEAKER on the last day before her cohort departs for their two-week internships with employers, announces this next phase of their educational journey as if she is announcing the start of a stock car race: "Put on your seat belt and ride out the ride!" Just a few minutes before, Training Futures cofounder and trainer Susan Craver used a similar image of a car journey to a new place. "There is a wise person within you who has these hopes, dreams, and vision. Keep talking with this person. Know also that there is a 'public me' and a 'private me.' We're taking the 'public me' on the road!"

At nine a.m. on the following Monday, all thirty-one of these students reported to employers' offices throughout Northern Virginia for the first day of their internships. On their internships, they test-drove their new skills and the new public selves that they had shaped during their first fifteen weeks at TF. Tenia read the letter she wrote to herself fifteen weeks ago: "I'm here to change my life and make myself self-sufficient. I want to leave this earth with something left that will help youth . . . Sometimes in the past, I haven't liked God's decisions, but these obstacles remind us what we're supposed to do with our lives."

As mentioned in chapter 3, each participant writes a letter to themselves during their first week at TF. The exercise asks participants to write a note describing why they chose to enroll in the program and what their goals are, and stating their commitment to persisting and completing the program. The letters are immediately sealed in envelopes and forgotten. After fifteen weeks, participants open the envelopes to read their letters again. This Letter to Self exercise is part of holding oneself accountable to the wise person within, and it reinforces the message of staying true to the hopes, dreams, and visions that led each student to embark on a journey beyond the familiar, rather than giving in to the fears of an unfamiliar journey. Some letters reflect an internal tug of war between doubts based on past difficulties and a compelling vision and determination to move forward in one's transformational journey, as the two examples that follow illustrate.

> Sometimes when I interviewed [for jobs], I found myself being somebody I'm not, rather than letting who I am shine. —*Latrice*

> I got this chance after many trials. I promise to work hard to fulfill my wish and change my life. —*Yodit*

When facing the prospect of performing new tasks in a new and different work environment—and in front of new coworkers and supervisors, as well—confronting a wellspring of fear is understandable and expected. Because of such stark changes, many participants like Latrice feel unsure of themselves when playing this new role. Beneath the fears of change, however, there is also the wise person within, as voiced by Tenia and Yodit, who knows that facing obstacles and trials is part of the journey toward a new vision.

This chapter describes the process of reintegration as students progress toward the end of their current transformation. We explore in depth three specific parts of the change process that students are experiencing: trying on new roles, building competence and self-confidence, and reintegration into one's life.[1] At the end of the chapter, we provide suggestions for immediate actions that readers can take to explore these parts of the transformation process, deepen their understanding, and identify ways that community college professionals can support students within their specific roles.

TRYING ON NEW ROLES

Julia, a TF graduate speaking on opening day to a new cohort: "The only skill I had was as a mother. I had never worked and didn't know computers. I thought, 'How can I study at my age?' . . . Challenge yourself and give yourself a try."

Imagine a motivated student who envisions herself as a particular kind of professional. She sits in a classroom and at home studying textbooks, completing homework assignments, and preparing for tests. She desperately wants to become that professional, but she just does not feel it yet. She can answer questions in class and perform well on tests, but she cringes at the thought of applying for jobs because she feels that all she has is book learning. What if the potential employer asks her specific questions about software programs used to do the job? What will she say if the interviewer prompts her with behavior-based interview questions that require her to talk about real experiences she has had? Further, there is the mortifying thought of showing up for the first day at a job with no real idea of the work that will be expected of her or how to do that work. Those who have worked with such students can probably recall examples of good students who got a great job offer, exactly the kind they had studied for, and yet turned it down. These seemingly mystifying cases might be understood through the lens of transformational learning, as could the thought exercise above about the student with book learning but no related job or workplace cultural experiences.

There is a big difference between learning course material, especially as traditionally taught in a college classroom, and becoming a professional. In order to accomplish the latter, students must at some point step out of their comfort zones and into their new roles. For students from historically underserved backgrounds, this leap into a new social role may include additional learning that historically served students do not have to navigate. The transition exists for everyone, and part of that transition is trying on the new role even though students do not feel authentic in it yet.

We use the term *trying on* to reflect the fact that these new social roles feel tentative and foreign. In the transformation process, it is a common phenomenon for people to try on new social roles. It is as if they need to start playing the part even though they feel like a fake or that they are not really who they are pretending to be. This section explores the importance of stepping out of one's comfort zone into new social roles, illustrates what the experience looks like through the eyes of some students, and discusses ways that community colleges can support students as they engage in this important part of the transformation process.

Public Me and Private Me

The difference between the public self and the private self is often much more pronounced for historically underserved students. Learning the norms of a hoped-for profession often includes their having to learn the norms of white, middle-class America, upon which the norms of higher education are based. One of the most basic norms is the English that they speak. Students often engage in a process of *code-switching* as they float between different social worlds. Code-switching is a term used in linguistics to refer to the way speakers of multiple languages shift between their different languages when talking—not just in the words, but in the rules and principles of the language, such as sentence structure or word order. We use the term to refer to switching between different cultural norms, speech patterns, and so forth that exist among the many subcultures in any country.

In elementary school, for example, many students from historically underserved backgrounds face additional learning challenges because the English they have learned while growing up is different from the dialect used and valued by the educational system. Rebecca Wheeler describes a typical situation:

> When African American students write *I have two sister and two brother, My Dad jeep is out of gas,* or *My mom deserve a good job,* teachers traditionally diagnose "poor English" and conclude that the students are making errors with plurality, possession, or verb agreement. In response, teachers correct the students' writing and show them the "right" grammar. Research has amply demonstrated that such traditional correction methods fail to teach students the Standard English writing skills they need.[2]

These students are speaking Black English Vernacular (BEV), a rule-based, structurally valid linguistic system that is not objectively better or worse than Standard English (SE); it is just different.[3] However, SE is the common dialect used and expected in higher education and in most higher-paying professional settings, and the use of BEV has often resulted in negative attitudes and lower expectations from teachers (and likely workplace recruiters and the like), which in turn has resulted in lower academic performance by those students.[4]

People from racially minoritized backgrounds often get accused of "acting white" when they display some of the cultural words, mannerisms, and syntax of higher education in their home neighborhoods. Students do not have to—and we feel *should* not have to—abandon the cultural norms and dialect with which they grew up. They often do, however, need to learn the expected cultural norms and dialect of their future workplace. In short, when historically underserved students are trying on new social roles, they may need to learn a wider range of tacit norms than their historically served classmates do. Students often need to be immersed in the culture and tasks of their hoped-for profession in order to get comfortable in it and learn the unwritten, unspoken rules and norms of the profession. Research has shown, however, that making the tacit more explicit can make a big difference in the learning outcomes of students.

Learning SE is an important example, and we use it here because there has been a lot of research on how to teach SE to students who speak BEV. However, we are not saying that teaching SE to community college students is essential. It is important for some professions, such as those in which interacting with customers is a large part of the job, if employers expect their employees to use SE. But the larger point is that there are many tacit norms expected in almost every profession. Program faculty need to diagnose and articulate what those tacit norms are within a professional field of study and then design the learning environment with both tacit and explicit experiences to help students learn those norms. And there needs to be training in code-switching prior to immersive experiences, such as internships, so that those experiences can help students try on their new professional roles and the codes and tacit norms needed, rather than feeling even more out-of-place in the workplace environment.

But how can tacit norms be taught? To explain, we draw on research conducted with elementary school students from racially minoritized groups on how explicitly learning to code-switch helped them. At the heart of the teaching techniques found to be effective in teaching SE to speakers of BEV is the underlying premise that speakers of BEV are not making errors and are certainly not intellectually or educationally deficient. Rather, they are simply speaking a different dialect. And using the proverbial red pen to highlight mistakes in the use of SE is not an effective way of teaching it.

Wheeler describes the work of a grade school teacher, Rachel Swords, who employed an effective process of teaching SE as a dialect.[5] First, Swords began with the following four premises: English comes in different varieties; each variety is structured, rule-governed and grammatical; we choose language features to fit the time, place, audience, and communicative purpose; and language is not "correct or incorrect," "right or wrong," but instead works or doesn't work in a particular setting.

Building on these premises, she helped students understand how everyone acts and speaks differently in different environments. Specifically, she led students to realize how they speak differently in informal (such as a neighborhood) and formal (such as in church) environments. Then, she created *contrasting analysis* tables in which the rules and structure of informal dialects (such as BEV) are explicitly contrasted with the SE dialect used in most formal environments. For instance, a common difference between BEV and SE is how plurality is shown. Swords showed that in informal usage, one might say, "I have two dog"—whereas in formal usage it would be, "I have two dogs." After several examples, she helps students see the embedded rules for each dialect. In informal usage, plurality is shown through number words (as with "two dog"), as well as in context clues elsewhere in the sentence and paragraph, or simply through common knowledge. In contrast, in formal usage (that is, Standard English), plurality is shown by adding the letter *s* to the end of a word.

By approaching teaching from the premise of code-switching between dialects, and by explicitly teaching students how to code-switch, she accomplished stunning results. Before implementing this approach in her third-grade classroom, Swords saw a thirty-point difference in the standardized test scores between her white and African American students. In her first year using this approach, her African American students performed just as well as her white students in English and history, and performed higher in math and science. Four years after that, she had 100 percent of her African American students pass the state's year-end standardized test.[6] These remarkable results emanate from a respectful approach (approaching the teaching of SE from the perspective of different dialects rather than assuming "incorrect" English) that uses the technique of making the tacit explicit (teaching code-switching between dialects).

To illustrate what this might look like in a community college classroom, here is a story from Susan Craver about how TF approached their Business Communication course.

We opened by discussing the rightful place of dialects alongside by-the-book English. We evolved a lesson plan which was fun on the surface but designed to give permission to use "business" English at Training Futures. First, we would ask how many trainees spoke two languages, on to three, four . . . The English-speaking trainees always looked sheepish at this point until the instructor said that everyone in the class spoke at least two languages. Then someone always said, "Oh! You must mean my slang." We then suggested that the two languages could be called Standard or "by-the-book" English and Non-Standard or personal English. Then we had the class brainstorm their favorite slang words or phrases. We flipped some of the phrases into "straight-up" English if the non-native English speakers didn't know them. It was always fun, which then set up the lesson that slang was fun, rich and dramatic. Then we asked who in the public eye almost always spoke Non-Standard English (actors, comedians, rappers, ethnic community speakers . . .) and Standard English (newscasters, public speakers, teachers . . .). When we asked "Why?" We clarified that one was to entertain and personalize and the other was to reach and inform a broad, diverse audience (like the business world.)

This really was grounded when we asked the trainees to write an indignant letter to a company which had not delivered an expensive mail-ordered item and to let their non-standard English fly. Then we had them flip it into standard or business English. It was great fun when the trainees read the two letters out loud. When asked what would happen if they sent the non-standard letter, they knew that the letter would not be taken seriously and probably be tossed after the first sentence. If they wanted to receive their order or a refund, they were clear that they better use standard English. We could then make the transition into why speak standard English in the workplace and why use Training Futures as a time to get comfortable speaking that version of their multiple languages. We could then bring out signs which said "Standard English Spoken Here" and have this practice seen not as judgmental but part of a purposeful, results-oriented journey.[7]

Immersive Pedagogies

It is important to create opportunities whereby students can hone their skills at code-switching in an immersive environment. By *immersive*, we refer to internships, clinical experiences, service learning, apprenticeships, and similar work-based methods, placing students in situations where they can apply their learning in authentic situations. In addition to gaining practice in code-switching, immersive pedagogies allow students to translate knowledge learned in the higher education context to a real work environment, start creating a professional network, and make themselves more marketable by building their resume. They allow students to try on their new professional roles, an essential function in their overall process of transformation, while still in school.

> On my internship, they trusted me more once they saw I was able to do more . . .When you get out and see how you can perform on the job, you will see how much you learned. —*Ines, a TF graduate speaking on a grad panel*

In a review of fifty-seven peer-reviewed articles, Gisela Vélez and Gabriela Giner found that the most consistent benefits of internships to students related to improved employment opportunities, improved skills and competencies, and career exploration.[8] Interestingly, among the specific benefits under these broader categories, they found that internships helped students strengthen their social skills and reduced reality shocks upon entering the workplace. We believe one underlying reason for these specific benefits stems from the development and learning of the tacit norms of the workplace in a given discipline or profession. Skills and competencies are improved because students get the opportunity to use them in authentic work settings, thus getting a sense for the nuance and applicability of their coursework. And they strengthen their social skills and reduce reality shocks because they acclimate, at least a little bit, to the unique social norms of that profession.

There are, of course, more effective and less effective ways to structure immersive learning environments. In the fifty-seven articles, there were four common research findings regarding effective internships. They were: having challenging assignments, greater autonomy, quality mentoring, and ongoing feedback. These design elements do not happen automatically. It takes planning and coordination between the college and workplace to ensure that students have prerequisite knowledge and skills so they will be able to work somewhat independently on challenging assignments, as well as to ensure that students will receive effective mentoring and feedback during their internship.

New Roles

This process of considering and trying on new roles in the job search process is a two-way street. In addition to students, prospective employers who may prefer hiring candidates that fit a specific image or with direct previous experience in a similar role may also face a mental journey when trying on a different type of candidate. An association executive who hired a TF graduate for a receptionist position described her thought process in considering a new type of recruit. At first, she admitted that she "simply wasn't interested" in interviewing an inexperienced candidate from a training program. Then, the TF staff recommended that she interview a former hairdresser named Marie. "I was very frustrated that I would have to do the interview . . . frustrated up to the point when she came in, that is." Marie "had a beautiful smile, and we had a very positive interview." After this experience, the executive reflected on similar things that both a hairdresser and receptionist do: "She greets customers; she has to communicate with them . . . she has to maintain the demeanor we were looking for." And the executive remembered why there was a receptionist opening in the first place: the previous receptionist had attendance problems and was let go. Marie, however, had completed a five-month training program without ever once being late, much less absent. "That's commitment," the executive concluded, which confirmed her decision to hire Marie.

The new receptionist job at a non-profit association wasn't what Marie had pictured either. She was hoping for a position in a technology company. However, she had begun to assess her skills and interests during the program, so when the receptionist opportunity came up, she recognized that the role of a receptionist was one that seemed to fit. "I didn't have a lot of computer skills," Marie confessed later. But "I'm a people person, and I smile a lot," an important asset for a receptionist, and one that the hiring executive immediately noticed. "I felt like I had the job when I left the interview," Marie added. It was "the attitude I had; it sold."

Immersive Experiences

The Association of American Colleges and Universities published a list of and rationale for "high-impact practices" almost a decade ago.[9] And although the rationale they offer does not use our terminology, many of those practices are especially relevant to the purposes of helping students try on new social roles by making the tacit explicit and by immersing students in authentic learning situations. Some of the practices they recommend are described next.

Internships Internships are a great way to help immerse students in authentic work environments related to their career aspirations and field of study. Colleges must obviously work with local employers to find and coordinate internship opportunities, but they should take this coordination further in order to provide the most effective experience possible. This includes determining the prerequisite knowledge and skills that internship employers expect students to have, so students can engage in relatively autonomous work that is beneficial to their learning as well as to the employer. Another important aspect of an effective internship is a mechanism for feedback and mentoring. Colleges can do their part in promoting an effective internship experience by encouraging students to actively learn from it, possibly through required assignments, journaling, and similar reflective exercises.

Service Learning Another immersive pedagogy is service learning, which is designed to help students apply their learning by analyzing and solving real problems in the local community. Similar to internships, service learning is a structured learning experience that is purposefully outside the classroom and in authentic, problem-based situations. In most service learning courses, there is an explicit focus on reflection on the experience, usually in a classroom environment, where students periodically meet with faculty to talk about the community problems they are trying to address, as well as about what the students are learning as they engage in the process.

Apprenticeships Beyond internships and service learning, the immersive work-based learning method that has gathered the most momentum in recent years, due in part to federal and state policy and funding emphasis, is apprenticeships. Once thought of as the domain primarily of unions and the building trades, apprentice-ships have expanded far beyond the trades in recent years, with new employer-sponsored apprenticeships in health care, IT, bank-ing and finance, and other fields. Apprenticeships blend work-based learning under the direction of a trained mentor with related technical instruction that is often delivered by a community col-lege. College-delivered training programs need to be carefully co-ordinated with immersive on-the-job experiences, a challenge that many community college professionals have grappled with. For historically underserved students from low-income households, the appeal of earning an immediate paycheck, free tuition in many apprenticeship programs that are funded by employers, and the acculturation that comes with on-the-job mentoring are especially attractive features. Apprenticeship programs offer a learning pro-cess in which trying on new roles is expected within a sequenced learning process that begins with easier and less risky work tasks and progresses naturally toward more complex ones over time. For example, in 2016, Grand Rapids Community College, in Mich-igan, established a Medical Assistant registered apprenticeship program with local hospitals that had a need for a more diverse workforce. By partnering with local nonprofits, the college at-tracted over 400 prospective program applicants at program intake events. Enrolled students of color rose from 3 percent for previous nonapprenticeship Medical Assistant programs to 25 percent in the most recent cohorts of the apprenticeship program.[10]

Dress for Success Incorporating workplace dress and gear into the educational setting can also be important. When performing labs or other simulated work, asking students to have the appropriate attire and equipment not only gives them a more fully immersive experience, but can also help them progress toward a professional self-image when they see themselves wearing and using the gear of the profession. Some programs prepare students for occupations that generally come with required attire and gear, such as hospital scrubs and lab coats; construction site hardhats, tools, and boots; and chefs' hats, coats, and knives. College programs can make this attire available early in a program, provide support for low-income students to acquire it, and ask students to wear and use their gear in labs and other work-based learning activities. TF has a mandatory professional dress code, which begins the week following participants' visit to the program's volunteer-run clothing closet to be outfitted with new professional wardrobes. After this visit, participants are given an assignment to write a thank-you letter to the volunteers who assisted them. These letters often speak to participants' reassessment of their self-image as prospective professionals and as people worthy of such kind attention, as several excerpts below indicate.

> Thank you for the beautiful clothes. Because of your patience and goodwill, I'm dressing the part of someone who is becoming successful. I enjoyed the experience of being in the company of humble women who were willing to be my personal shoppers. That was something I always wanted to experience and never had the money to.

> Thank you for the transformation . . . You helped me learn how to look great. Most of all, you helped me to find myself again. This was so helpful to me because I'm a mother of five. I've always dressed in t-shirts, shorts, or jeans. I've been a mother for so long I had forgotten about myself.

I know that I might not have all the coordination to put outfits together, but I got a wonderful start by some positive women that want me to be successful and look successful. I hope that in the future I can share my success, my time, my support, leadership and the same eagerness to help others that you all have showed me.

In this case, the affirmation of caring volunteers and the mirror itself—when participants see in their own reflection the results of their professional makeover—both function as critical mirrors that can help lead to a reassessment of their self-image as professionals. By helping to create positive images of students as professionals who are worthy of time and attention from caring volunteers, this experience also contributes to students' growing self-confidence that they are ready to step into new professional roles, which is the focus of the next section.

BUILDING COMPETENCE AND SELF-CONFIDENCE

As students gain necessary knowledge and skills, as well as experience trying on their new social roles, they start to build competence and self-confidence. For instance, one of the first learning modules on which TF participants focus is also the most tangible to observe: keyboarding. This skill is easily assessed and tracked by standard tests to measure typing speed and accuracy. During their first two weeks in the program, participants complete multiple demonstration tests to measure and chart their progress. During their supervisory group meeting at the end of the second week, Lucy excitedly reported rapid gains in typing speed from twenty-five to thirty-seven words per minute. Ghenet increased from thirty-nine to fifty-four.

A few who reported difficulties with keyboarding were busy unlearning old habits that can block progress. "I only used two fingers before," reported one trainee, who cited keyboarding as one of her challenges for the week. Dee, a beginner at the keyboard, found it easier to make quick progress.

"Keyboarding," says Craver, "is a metaphor for the tension between new me and old me. Some trainees have to unlearn old ways, but the payoff is almost immediate" for those who pursue this skill with discipline and daily practice. Saida is one of those. "I was up practicing my typing until one a.m.!" she exclaimed.

For adults who have not been in a formal learning environment for some time, having an opportunity to quickly experience success builds confidence as a learner that increases their motivation to learn more, as we saw above with Saida. When the achievement of an important job skill like keyboarding can be easily measured and observed (exceptional typing speed is a concrete productivity measure that can be placed directly onto a resume), the sense of skill mastery is unmistakable and can serve as validation that one is becoming a valuable professional. While this relatively quick and simple learning achievement may be an exception to what is more often a slower-motion process of learning, the keyboarding example from TF demonstrates how learning in the classroom and in immersive environments can translate into a growing sense of mastery and confidence in performing new roles. And this, of course, applies to much more than just keyboarding.

> On the first day here, I was the kind of person who couldn't talk with two people. When we had to introduce ourselves on the first day at Training Futures, I nearly had a heart attack. But . . . today [after fifteen weeks in the program], I felt like a totally different person. Now I can talk with 10,000 people. —*Tallat, TF graduate*

In the last PowerPoint presentation [I gave in class], I was able to just speak up without turning red. I was more confident. —*Shirley, TF graduate*

Hitting the Wall

A challenge that often arises with students can be described as "hitting the wall." This type of experience is what Craver was referring to when she announced to staff colleagues at a meeting midway into the term: "It looks like we're in breakdown." For several days, she listened to participants describe what hitting the wall feels like during the months-long transformational journey that is the TF program:

- "I can't remember what we're being taught in computers."
- "There's too many computer procedures for me to retain them all."
- "I'm afraid that I have a learning disability. Maybe I'm just meant to be a housewife."

This is the moment during the program when more challenging learning tasks begin to instill doubts about one's ability to succeed. Many older adult learners have been out of the classroom for some time, and they lack confidence in their abilities as a student in higher education. Others may have had painful experiences more recently—in high school or in a not-so-successful earlier attempt at college—that still feel like raw wounds. When doubts about one's abilities begin to arise, they can feed students' deeply embedded story lines of struggle, failure, victimization, or powerlessness. Students' overloaded minds shout out reasons why they cannot go on learning. The fears dredged up from past experiences in a new learning environment can easily become magnified and lead students to drop the course, stop attending, or to downshift into self-defeating behaviors that can further disrupt their learning progress.

Hitting the wall often includes a disruption in a student's sense of identity. As one TF student said: "As a stay-at-home mom for years, I lost myself. I didn't know who I was anymore." It can be easy to lose ourselves in the primary roles that we play in life. Even though there is nothing wrong with being a stay-at-home mom, for instance, when life events and decisions lead students back to school, it becomes evident how those roles have evolved into more than just roles; they turn into a sense of identity. And when students are in the midst of changing those roles, they often also begin to engage in deep questions about who they are and what their changing roles mean for their sense of identity.

Another part of this process tends to be an examination of their lives, particularly the elements of themselves and the events that have led them to where they currently are in life. One TF student, Connie, reflected:

> I've always made bad choices. For example, I applied and was accepted into Job Corps. For several weeks, I spent time with all my friends, like I was going away forever. When the day came to leave, I didn't show up for the bus. I had too much to drink the night before and had wrecked my car. My dad decided that I was not a good role model for the younger kids [in our family], so I moved out.

We have all made mistakes in our lives. It can be easy for students to look at mistakes they have made and make generalizations about themselves, such as Connie's assertion that she has "always made bad choices." She has probably also made a lot of good choices, but the narrative she has created about herself focuses on the negative.

Another way students wrestle with their identities is when they look deeply at their current situation and what they are trying to do to change their lives. As Amani, another TF student, said in her graduation remarks:

[School] has helped me deal with my past, because that is what was holding me back. To live life operating out of fear is most detrimental to one's soul. It is the worst kind of self-destruction, and it brings about an internal isolation from the rest of the world. Thank God I'm on the road to recovery with dealing with myself and realizing that I had to first confront my past in order to move on with my future.

Hitting the wall is one way of describing the experience of community college students during this phase of transformation, when their old identities and ways of being collide with the emerging "new me" that is in the process of becoming, forcing a reckoning between the two competing images. In the midst of all the changes going on in their lives—in their external lives and, more important, in their internal lives—students inevitably begin looking inward. They try to make sense of themselves, their past (how they got where they are), and their current experiences. As in the quotes above, this examination can become especially intense when the learning required in classes becomes difficult and/or when students are midway through the term and, seeing how difficult classes have been so far, become overwhelmed at the prospect of finishing the term, much less the overall program.

To support students during times when they are likely to hit the wall, it is useful to remind them of the reasons they chose to pursue their education in the first place. The Letter to Self activity is designed to do just that. It begins in the first week of the program, ideally after some initial community-building activities and discussion, in which participants get a signal that the course or program is more than just skills training. Students are instructed to write three specific goals that they hope to achieve through the program, and then to write words of encouragement describing what they will do to support themselves to successfully complete the program. The letters are placed in a sealed envelope and given to the instructor. Months later, at a moment in the program when a reminder of these goals and self-support strategies are needed, the letters are returned to students, and group members are encouraged to share some of their letters. For this activity, educators need to discern when in a program (or a course) students are likely to be at their lowest point in terms of confidence and motivation. Its purpose is to remind students of their reasons for committing to the time and challenges of obtaining a college credential, and seeing their own words as well as hearing from other participants can help bolster their confidence and motivation when it is likely to be flagging.

Impostor Syndrome

Another challenge that commonly arises with students is "impostor syndrome."

> To some extent, of course, we are all impostors. We play roles on the stage of life, presenting a public self that differs from the private self we share with intimates and morphing both selves as circumstances demand. Displaying a façade is part and parcel of the human condition.[11]

One of the most difficult aspects of dramatic personal change is feeling like an impostor, or someone who is practicing deception under an assumed identity.[12] Historically underserved students are often unfamiliar with the core skills, insider knowledge, and unwritten rules expected in their new social roles, which exacerbates this sense of impostorship. As community college students strive to gain these capabilities, they are often impeded by deep, internalized beliefs that not only do they not belong in their new roles, but that they are inadequate to the tasks required, and that others are likely to spot their phoniness if they just look hard enough.

This phenomenon was articulated at least as early as 1978 when the term *impostor syndrome* was coined by Pauline Clance and Suzanne Imes in a study of 150 high performing women who, despite their objective successes, reported an internalized sense of intellectual phoniness, believing that their success was not really earned but rather was a result of luck and of others overestimating their abilities.[13] The terms impostor syndrome and impostor phenomenon have become ubiquitous in the research literature ever since then. Most people can probably relate to feelings of phoniness and inadequacy when adopting a new social role, and even a quick perusal on Google Scholar of these terms shows that seemingly every profession has its own version of the phenomenon.

Consider the feelings described by a newly promoted nurse, a familiar community college training occupation:

I keep thinking someone will figure out how much I really don't know and question whether I should've been given the position. Sometimes I feel like an imposter. When I mention this to my friends, they tell me to "fake it until you make it." But I'm not so sure about that![14]

For some people, these feelings of impostorship persist regardless of the passing of time or accrual of accomplishments; these individuals are beyond the purview of this book. Our focus here is on the temporary feelings of impostorship and inadequacy that are common when people begin new social roles, including that of becoming a college student and beginning a new professional career. Consider how an underrepresented student must feel in a new college professional studies program, who faces a double dose of impostor syndrome—as both a new college student and a soon-to-be new professional. These feelings can become real barriers to persistence if they become too pronounced.

Stephen Brookfield described the feelings of impostorship that he has seen when trying to help community college students develop the skills and habits of critical thinking:

> Impostorship occurs when students feel, at some deeply embedded level, that they possess neither the talent nor the right to become critical thinkers. When asked to undertake a critical analysis of ideas propounded by people seen as experts, learners often feel that to do so smacks of temerity and impertinence.[15]

Nancy Schlossberg wrote about this phenomenon in terms of *marginality*, or a sense of not fitting in (she contrasts it with *mattering*).[16] Everyone, she says, has contexts in which they simply do not feel as if they are genuinely a part of the community. It can manifest as simply as people in that community not talking with or smiling at you. People who are marginalized do not feel as if they are participating intimately in the cultural life and traditions of that particular social context. This sense of being marginal, she claims, can lead to increased irritability, depression, and self-consciousness, especially for new students. Students, she claims, may begin sliding down a slippery slope of diminishing self-confidence, focusing on their failures and mistakes, diminishing their successes, and resulting in increased stress and anxiety.[17] They feel alienated from their new environment. If these feelings of inadequacy, falseness, stress, anxiety, and alienation persist, they can become a real impediment to students' persistence, completion of their credentials, and career aspirations.

There are several techniques that can help students move through and past these feelings of impostorship. One recommendation is drawn from a study by Mary Topping in 1983, in which she demonstrated how it can be helpful for students to understand that this is a common phenomenon, and that the thoughts and feelings the students are experiencing are normal.[18]

In a review of the literature on the impostor phenomenon, Queena Hoang concluded that a powerful technique to help students overcome it is to help shift their focus from others' perceptions of them to their own internal motivations for pursuing an education.[19] She recommends that intrinsic motivation is manifest in thoughts such as:

- "I want to receive that degree. I won't give up and have too much pride to walk away."
- "If I can do this, I will be able to help others in the future and work with people as motivated as I am."
- "I can be the voice of other People of Color who do not have the opportunities like I do."

The suggestions by Hoang demonstrate that instilling a higher purpose helps students persist even when they feel incompetent or like a fraud. Therefore, it can be beneficial to help students articulate and focus on their reasons for pursuing a college education. Exercises that do this amount to a purposeful reframing of the way students experience, interpret, and react to the challenges and feelings of impostorship that are natural when people embark on a path to a new social role.

Another suggestion by Hoang was to provide mentors for new students from among alumni or students nearing graduation. These near-peer mentors can relate to what new students are feeling and help them see that feelings of impostorship are common, as well as serve as role models as someone who has been through and overcome those feelings.

> My skills were really outdated. I was able to learn about Microsoft Office Suite at the same time that I was getting a lot of positive reinforcement from people who believed in me. —*Barbara, a former stay-at-home mom returning to work in a law firm after completing TF*

Self-Efficacy and Fading Supports

In his TF graduation speech, Miguel described a lifetime of hard manual labor since the age of ten, interrupted in his twenties by an unexpected illness that left him feeling hopeless.

> Two years ago, I was sick, with no job, no health insurance . . . I felt lost and defeated. . . . When I came in to interview [for the TF program], what a day that was for me. They told me I had potential! I started to believe in myself. Now I know that I can conquer any situation, good or bad.

In order for people to experience growth, they need both validation and challenge.[20] In his explanation of lifelong growth and development, Robert Kegan states that people need to feel validated that their current ways of thinking and being are legitimate, so that their energy can turn toward the adaptation and growth necessary to accommodate current challenges, rather than that energy being focused on defending and justifying their current ways of thinking and being. And yet, they need these new challenges to provide the impetus for growth. College offers plenty of challenges, but providing validation as a means of support for students does not automatically happen. Purposefully promoting self-efficacy is a key way of providing support.

One of the first challenges that many students face is a lack of self-efficacy as a college student. As discussed in chapter 1, Albert Bandura's concept of self-efficacy refers to people's beliefs about whether and to what extent they can achieve their goals and influence events in their lives.[21] We are reminded of Vincent Tinto's assertion that students arrive on campus with various levels of commitment, and that it increases or decreases based on the extent to which they feel academically and social integrated on campus.[22] Similarly, Laura Rendón, Romero Jalomo, and Amaury Nora speak of the need that students, especially historically underserved students, have for validation, which they define as processes that enable, confirm, and support students.[23] And they argue that this validation is especially important, even critical, at the beginning of the students' academic journeys. We believe that one of the key reasons why these enabling, confirming, and supporting endeavors are so critical—especially at the outset of students' college experience—is because they help bolster academic self-efficacy.

This model of actively facilitating student self-efficacy is sometimes referred to as *fading support*, which can be done any number of ways. The NOVA–TF partnership offers one example. For many years, until budget cuts reduced such outreach services, NOVA's Adult Career Pathways program provided a college success advisor who began working with students at the TF site during the program to learn about their career goals and, for those who were interested in immediately continuing their college studies, to jointly plan their follow-up studies at NOVA after completing TF. The initial cohort that received these ongoing advising services saw a jump in NOVA course enrollments from 18 percent of TF graduates to 46 percent.[24] Most often, students needed to focus on their new entry-level office administrative jobs, so their studies had to be coordinated around work and commuting schedules for their new jobs. The NOVA advisor worked with each interested student intensely during the transition to NOVA, with up to three advising meetings on-site at TF and continuing close contact via phone and email once the program ended. After one or two semesters of close and more frequent advising interactions, and after students had selected a program of study, demonstrated mastery of college processes such as course registration, and had at least one successful academic term post-TF, their assigned NOVA advisor backed off from more active guidance to allow students space to self-manage their studies, and checked in less frequently.

Mindset

We are particularly intrigued by the mindset work of Carol Dweck, a psychologist at Stanford University. Many community colleges have struggled, for example, to improve dismal success rates in developmental math, which is recommended to around half of all community college students. One national review of developmental math success rates found that less than half (45 percent) of students in the highest level of developmental math succeeded in completing their prescribed developmental math sequence, dropping to 17 percent for those at the lowest level.[25]

One promising experimental study of 288 community college developmental math students succeeded in cutting the course failure rate by 50 percent by using a thirty-minute mindset assignment at the beginning of the course. In the experiment, students were randomly assigned either to a control group that read a generic article about the brain, or an experimental group that read a short science-based article describing how practice in math can "grow" one's brain. The latter group was also asked to write a short mentoring letter to future students describing the article. The intent of this design for the experimental group was to change how students thought of themselves as learners of math. It is commonly said that people are naturally good or bad at math. The problem with this belief is that when students have struggled with math over much of their academic lives, they usually attribute those struggles to a genetic predisposition that cannot be changed. (This belief also hurts students who have had success in math, because when they encounter math that does not come as naturally to them, they often give up because they have seemingly reached the end of their natural ability to do it.) Therefore, this experiment sought to help students reframe math as something anyone can do and to convince them that the brain changes because of math. Therefore, even if they have struggled with math in the past, it is not because they are naturally bad at math, but rather that they simply need to do more math in order to get good at it.

The course dropout rate for the experimental group was less than half of that for the control group: 9 percent versus 20 percent.[26] A similar study with over 800 community college students found a 14 percent improvement in developmental math grades associated with a mindset intervention.[27] Experiments such as these demonstrate how helping students build their academic self-efficacy, in this case through mindset interventions, can yield promising results.

Providing the developmental prompts of challenges (encouraging students to devote more time and effort to learning) and supports (such as giving assignments that can result in quick and visible successes if students expend the effort) is possible. For historically underserved students, as described repeatedly in this book, there are already plenty of challenges presented by most every aspect of their college experience. They, like all students, will need to learn and develop so they can rise to the level of those challenges. Therefore, we recognize the need to provide critical feedback to students so they can increase their effort, when applicable, and/or improve their skills. To be clear, we are not advocating for a lowering of standards. Rather, we are arguing that support needs to precede any efforts to provide additional challenges beyond what are already present.

In order to help students learn and grow from the challenges presented in college, it is important, in addition to providing mechanisms of support, to give feedback. "To be effective, assessments must be frequent, early, and formative."[28] As Tinto's quotation asserts, such feedback should be given early and often, and with the intent of helping students learn. We believe the way to approach feedback is to begin with early successes to build confidence, and this is especially important in the gateway courses that students take early in their college experience. As described above, at TF there is an early emphasis on a specific part of the curriculum (keyboarding) where practice quickly pays off with visible and significantly improved results. It is no accident that keyboarding is taught early in the curriculum; it is not absolutely required before other skills are taught. It is offered in the beginning because the quick success usually experienced in keyboarding builds confidence in learners who may have doubted their ability to succeed in postsecondary education. There is a balance to be found in having high expectations and still providing small successes to help build academic self-efficacy.

One method to help find this balance is providing formative assessments early and often. Formative assessments are intended to help students and faculty gauge the students' current level of knowledge or skill proficiency for the purposes of promoting student learning. As such, they are low stakes, meaning that students need to know that these assessments do not heavily impact their grade. And, it is usually beneficial for the earliest formative assessments to be geared to measure the student's level of effort rather than their ability to master more difficult or challenging material. The latter may set students up for failure if they are asked to immediately perform at high levels on a course's more difficult assignments or materials.

Inevitably, assessments need to provide feedback on more challenging learning objectives, and therefore they will need to critique and give advice in addition to positive reinforcement. Students need to receive this critical feedback on low-stakes assessments early in a semester, and in a way that does not affect their overall performance in the class, so that they can make changes to turn things around. If a student is a quarter of the way through the semester before realizing that their efforts and/or key understandings are not what they need to be, then the class has done them a disservice. At that point they may have dug a hole for themselves that will be too difficult to get out of. However, if there are frequent mini assessments, students are able to see the level of effort that is going to be required of them, and they can internalize it early in the term. The conversation goes something like this: "We are one week into the semester, and this assignment was due. This is not the quality that is eventually needed, and this assignment will receive a poor grade. However, this grade is okay. We can move past it. In fact, I forgive the lowest grade. But it is what it is so you know the quality and rigor that this course expects of you." And then the instructor works with the student to help them learn the key things that are holding them back. And, because it is so early in the semester, the student is not yet far behind and has time to benefit from the feedback given.

To make this work, faculty have to do these mini assessments early and often so students receive a fast feedback loop. This contrasts sharply with the method of using summative assessments: perhaps two, three, or four assessments the entire semester, all of which have a high impact on students' grades and are designed to test whether they learned the material—but often after it is too late for that assessment to really help learning. This method hurts the academic self-efficacy of many students and does not contribute much to their learning.[29]

Student Testimony

Each TF cohort concludes with a graduation event. At the event, invited guests—including volunteers, internship sponsors, local officials, and funding representatives—celebrate and honor cohort members' achievements as a group and individually. It is a rite of passage ceremony that tells them, "You belong." A highlight of the graduation is the two graduate speakers who share their transformational stories from the podium. These stories often recount participants' fears and challenges at the beginning and how their learning achievements snowballed into growing confidence in their new professional capabilities. Several graduation stories, excerpted below, illustrate these narratives:

> In his presentation, Victor admitted that he was unsure that he could make the jump into a professional career in office administration. "I worked for years as a cook and a waiter. I had little knowledge of offices. Never in a million years did I think I could

do this." Then, he announced the news that he had just accepted a job offer as an administrative assistant. Victor described how the training program built his confidence so that he could envision success in a new professional career in a completely different professional setting than the familiar world of restaurant work. "If you think you can, then you can [succeed in a new job]," he said. "And if you think you can, then you are right."

Sonia, a returning student, was anxious about her ability to succeed in higher education. "I had been out of school for twenty years. At Training Futures, there was homework, tests, and even spelling bees . . . I thought, 'What have I gotten myself into now?' The next thing I knew, I was well on my way to seeing myself as a success in any field I might choose."

Shannon cited the people and environment at Training Futures as key to reclaiming a positive outlook about her life prospects. "It turned my life around, because I'd been around negative people all my life. I knew I'd be changed because there were so many positive people." Shannon told of her daily struggles just to get her family of four children to where they needed to be each morning in order to get to Training Futures on time, but she didn't give up, especially after "everyone convinced me that I could do things I didn't think I could do." She announced that she was weighing two job offers.

Graduation events are among the many ways that the program continually celebrates the learning achievements of participants, helping to build their confidence as learners and as professionals. Stories such as those shared by Victor, Sonia, and Shannon also illustrate how the staff's strengths-based assessments of participants' potential and the formation of a positive support community create a safe space where people can recover confidence in their abilities by rising to meet academic and workplace performance tests.

REINTEGRATION INTO ONE'S LIFE

The transformation process should result in the person eventually finding themselves in a new state of normalcy with their revised meaning perspectives. An important part of this new normal is that individuals' behaviors align with their changed perspective. Community college students, for instance, will engage in meaningful activities within their new school context as they progress through their transformation. These activities can range from appropriate self-management, such as planning ahead for large projects or getting adequate sleep, to demonstrations of mastery of their new roles, such as being a good study partner or engaging in campus leadership activities.

Not only are these students adapting well to their new context, many scholars argue that this process of transformation also helps them develop in important ways. They may develop a more internalized sense of self, priorities, and goals, and thus have less of a need to receive validation from others.[30] This type of growth and development will manifest in ways such as students placing more importance on their own reasons for engaging in certain activities than on what other people think about their activities. Students who do not fully transition may therefore continue to struggle to manage their time, priorities, relationships, and other concurrent stressors of college life, and they may not develop a clear reason for pursuing their education. Having successfully adapted to the college environment and received validation in numerous ways throughout that process, students may develop more confidence in their ability to handle new and challenging tasks and adopt a more optimistic attitude toward life and their ability to succeed in future endeavors.[31]

An Imaginal Education

The TF program focuses especially on shifting participants' images of themselves as professionals through a teaching method called Imaginal Education, which is designed to promote transformation.[32] Similar to Mezirow, this model proposes that people often operate out of internalized images of themselves. If, for example, those deeply embedded images shift from portraying victimhood and powerlessness to portraying empowerment and self-agency, then new behaviors will follow to shape a new phase of their lives. One clue about participants' readiness to continue adapting and learning to make their way in a new environment are the images that they use in describing themselves. Below are several excerpts from TF participants' stories that illustrate their shift in self-image in various ways:

> Deep in our heart, everyone wishes for a home. By home, I mean a place where you belong, are respected, loved and trained to be responsible. My desire for a home has been strong all of my life because my mother gave me to an orphanage. Later some relatives kept me and treated me like a prisoner. . . . From the first day at Training Futures, I knew I had finally found a real home. What a joy for me after so many years. I still hear [my trainers'] voices whispering encouragement and advice in my ear. That is the gift of finally finding a home and family at Training Futures where people have believed in me. — *"Home," by Phuong*

> Although I'm a father of two and twenty-one years old, before Training Futures, I was still a kid on the inside holding back my

potential. I always did just enough to get by. . . . I am ready to take on the world this time, not a fresh eighteen-year-old kid, but a new person. A new person loaded up on confidence, armed with a new set of skills and a semester of college. — *"Not a Kid Anymore," by José*

I never thought that the rainy season in my life would start one month [after arriving in Northern Virginia]. But, I became homeless together with my special daughter. The ground was my floor and the sky was my roof. No money. No food. And no friends. . . . Though my circumstances pointed me to be a failed person, I decided to be successful, and that Training Futures would be my rainbow. — *"The Rainy Season," by Maria*

Each of these participants' stories features different contrasting images—of home, youth, and a rainstorm, but each shows a dramatic perspective shift from the earlier to the later transformed image. Through many different programmatic elements, TF provides opportunities for participants to shift their images of themselves and their place in a new world of work. As their self-image changes, the newly learned attitudes, behaviors, and personal communication that accompany one's new image or perspective are more likely to stick.

Identity: Current and Imagined

A key part of this final phase is the development of the individual's sense of an identity in alignment with their new life context. The development of identity is a common theme in any of the various disciplines that talk about significant personal change.

My sense of identity [was] stripped away as I went from one foster home to another. But I've always had this fire burning in me to do more, to be more, to succeed in life . . . Life's twists and turns have taken bits and pieces of me, and what Training Futures has done is to put back all of those pieces. I'm a totally new and improved Sandra. Before, I was just surviving, and now I'm focusing on the future . . . My fire is burning bright. —*Sandra, in her TF graduation speech*

Most modern understandings of identity stem from Erik Erikson's work in the 1950s, wherein he described identity as the combination of 1) the experience of being the same throughout all the various situations in life, and 2) how we wish to present ourselves to the world. Most theorists who have expanded on Erikson's work have placed a greater emphasis on the social nature of identity (the idea that identity only really develops and exists in interaction with others). And in a world where one needs to change at a deep, personal level in order to adapt to a constantly changing environment, the work of identity formation (and *reformation*) is an ongoing endeavor.

> For the new generations growing up since the 1980s, the task or duty of creating, maintaining, and changing their own identities has become increasingly important. Who am I? Who do I want to be? How can I fulfill my dreams? The possibilities may be great and never ending for some. But for others, the many choices can become a strain, a continuous demonstration of their insufficient individual capacity to make things function. It is very difficult to obtain so much contact with one's identity that it can function as a yardstick for making the right choices when things constantly change.[33]

For community college faculty and administrators, the crucial idea here is that for many students, the task of changing their identities to match a new situation can be an arduous one because so many important changes are happening in a relatively short period of time. And if students' sense of identity does not shift to accommodate their new social roles, they are much more likely to drop out of school and return to a social role that aligns with their identity.

Until a student's identity evolves to that of being a college student, they will likely expect to perform poorly in school and eventually leave before completing a credential. Belief trumps desire—or, said differently, belief that something will happen is often more powerful than the desire for it not to happen. To help students make this important transition, it can be useful to think about identity change using Hazel Markus and Paula Nurius's concept of possible selves, as introduced in chapter 2.[34] Possible selves are the images people have of who they expect to become, who they hope to become, and who they are afraid to become. This last category is especially important because if the individual believes that this feared possible self will likely happen, then the image will drive behavior that leads to it. For instance, if a student fears becoming a college dropout, and fixates on that fear, they may act in ways that lead to this outcome even though they do not really want it to happen.

However, this feared possible self can also drive positive behavior if the individual does not view it as inevitable but instead uses it as a motivational force to become something else. Because of the powerful influence of what students believe will happen, we have found it more useful to help students focus on the possible selves they want to become. If students are prompted and encouraged to envision themselves succeeding, they will be more likely to engage in behaviors that lead to that success—and the more they engage in appropriate behaviors for their new social role, the more likely it is that their sense of identity will expand to include these new roles.

Changing one's identity is no easy feat, and often it cannot be accomplished simply by willing the identity to become something new. Two powerful mechanisms to facilitate identity change are narratives and metaphors.

Mark Tennant, a leading scholar on identity and adult learning, writes about the various ways that identity can be understood and changed in adulthood.[35] One of these ways is what he calls the *narrative self*. Narratives are the stories we use to make sense of our lives and the world around us. They give a sense of coherence, continuity, and meaning to our lives. As such, they form an important part of our sense of identity. We often do not realize the narratives that we have created, but they nevertheless shape and define our experience of life.

There are cultural narratives that we adopt from the social environment in which we spend our childhood, and there are also personal narratives that we craft based on a relatively small number of memories and a whole host of assumptions. For example, according to Ai-Jen Poo and Eldar Shafir, in the United States there are three cultural narratives about poverty and economic mobility that are "widespread, inaccurate, mutually contradictory, and harmful."[36] These narratives are:

- People in poverty have no one to blame but themselves for their circumstances;
- People in poverty are helpless victims of a larger socioeconomic system in which they have no agency; and
- Truly exceptional "rags-to-riches" stories prove that the American dream is available to anyone willing to work hard enough for it.

Many historically underserved students use this story to understand their lives. But not only are these narratives not true, they are also not helpful. They serve to perpetuate social and economic disparities by placing the blame on poor people for being poor rather than on social institutions, policies, and norms that make it difficult to escape from poverty—or they remove the blame from poor people in a way that conveys that escaping from poverty is almost impossible. To make the problem worse, often faculty, staff, administration, and policy makers are using these same narratives. Their words, actions, and policies reinforce and keep these narratives alive, which makes it doubly difficult for students to see them as cultural myths rather than the truth of things. For example, a student whose initial experience on campus is the testing center where they discover that they are not college-ready may reinforce an internalized narrative that they are not good enough. If they are required to take developmental education courses, the college has also imposed a higher cost burden on them in the form of additional tuition for these courses, which may reinforce a worry that they cannot afford college. Luckily, changing one's narrative is relatively easy. The hardest part is realizing the underlying narratives that are in use. Once seen, they can be scrutinized and replaced with more accurate and/or more helpful narratives.

Another underlying mechanism that shapes the way students make sense of themselves and their experiences are metaphors.[37] Just like the narratives discussed above, humans use metaphors as a heuristic by which they interpret and make sense out of their experiences. They allow complex understandings, usually ones that would be difficult to fully articulate, to be understood by comparing them to something else. Much has been written about metaphors and their profound influence on human meaning-making, and some scholars have written specifically about the power of examining one's metaphors in order to enact deep, personal learning and change. [38]

> I used to work in a coffee shop on the first floor of a tall office building. I felt unimportant waiting on busy career people—like a mouse around elephants. Now, I walk into those office buildings in my suit with my new skills and confidence. In just four months, I am an elephant too! —*Anonymous, TF graduate speaking at graduation*

This quote is a great example of how metaphors are used instinctively in a person's automatic processes of making sense out of their experiences, as well as how they can be used to promote deep change. In saying that they she felt like a mouse around elephants, the speaker is naming her felt experience. There is not only a sense of unimportance in comparison to the "busy career people," but there is also a sense of scurrying around trying to keep them pleased, as well as one of danger of being stepped on by these more powerful beings. In this metaphor, the server and customer are not equals in different work roles, they are completely different species; there is an innate, genetic difference between them. A mouse will never be an elephant. Whether the person realizes the implications of this metaphor—and regardless if these assumptions hold up under scrutiny—this metaphor sends and reinforces these messages. The metaphor is a reflection of the assumptions being made about the situation, and it reinforces these and other embedded messages to the person using it.

In a study of breast cancer survivors, coauthor Chad Hoggan found three ways that metaphors were used during a process of personal change that led to an improved quality of life for the participants. [39] First, metaphors were used to name their experiences.

This is how the person in the above quote was using it: to name her experience working in a coffee shop serving "busy career people." It speaks, among other facets of the experience, to her feelings of being lesser than these customers.

Another way metaphors were used in the study was to uncover tacit ways of making meaning. In the mouse/elephant example, if the student realized she was using this metaphor, she could evaluate and unpack it to discover how she was making sense of her experiences. With that insight, she would be better able to evaluate the tacit assumptions embedded in the metaphor, might stop using this metaphor, and possibly could adopt another metaphor for her work at the coffee shop.

The third way that metaphors were used was to imagine new possibilities. This approach is embedded in the imaginal education method that TF used as the basis of their design. The idea is to encourage students to create meaningful and positive metaphors, in which the embedded assumptions are helpful and inspiring and prompt the student to persevere through the hard work required to make the changes in their lives that they want to make.

New Beginnings

As we conclude this chapter, we want to briefly revisit the purposes of our use of Mezirow's model of transformational learning. Obviously, the portrayal of the process of transformation that we have used to frame this book is simplified in that there are not clear beginnings and endings to it. As Hoggan, Kaisu Mälkki, and Fergal Finnegan point out, it would be simplistic to depict change as an isolated event.

> [A]lthough it is easier to talk about [transformational learning] as
> if there are finite beginnings and endings of the learning . . . it is

more accurate to talk about overlapping trajectories of transformation. Small instances of disorientation may begin a slow, cumulative yet strong process of change. Furthermore, the end of one change process is often a stimulus for something new. The resolution of a dilemma creates new dilemmas, especially as the learner interacts in a variety of social surroundings.[40]

Thus, we have students at this phase of the transformational learning process who are finally feeling a sense of normalcy in being a student, but at the same time the experiences they have had in school are likely causing them to question even more parts of their lives, and as they near completion of their credentials, they will have another transition into a new social role as they begin a career. This next transition holds the possibility of sparking another disorienting dilemma that leads to additional transformational learning outcomes. Life, with all its complexities and challenges, continues to move on. So we talk about this last phase of transformation with the caveat that the students' experiences of change do not end like a Hollywood movie. Hopefully, however, their transformational learning experience in community college will have prepared them to navigate future transitions and transformations.

ADDITIONAL APPLICATIONS

Peer Mentoring

At TF, stronger students who complete a learning exercise quickly are asked to coach or assist others who struggle. For example, in a course where students practice completing specified Microsoft Office tasks and formatting with actual documents, students who are more advanced computer users are seated next to those who are newer computer users, so that ongoing peer questions-and-answers and coaching can occur naturally in the classroom, and students are less dependent on a single instructor to answer questions. Another application of peer mentoring within a cohort program is to form "success teams" with small groups of four to six students. Success teams offer a forum where students can discuss their goals and challenges, and receive encouragement and guidance from others over time. Formed during class or orientation, and under the guidance of an instructor or advisor for a couple of initial sessions, success teams can then continue meeting on their own, or with lighter support, especially immediately before or after a class that they all attend.

Success Montage

Around ten weeks into the TF program (and sometimes during the job-search phase as well), students are directed to develop a Success Montage. In this activity, students paste onto poster board a composite self-portrait with pictures and text from magazines that depict where they see themselves as a result of the training program. The activity is carefully structured so that the montage is training related and depicts who and how students want to be as people who live with intention. For example, students have often used sayings like "go for more," "congratulations," or "dream it—do it," and pictures of successful businesspeople at computers, in meetings, climbing steps to the future, or standing in front of open doors. Some also choose pictures that symbolize success or happiness indirectly, such as a thumbs-up icon or light-filled nature scenes or bouquets of flowers. At the end of the creative exercise, students explain their success montages by talking with a group of peers about the pictures and sayings they chose and why they chose them. These are often heartfelt conversations that deepen the experience into a profound declaration of their future vision for their careers and lives. The montages can be placed on the training room wall before being taken home, but either way they are a powerful way of claiming the future and a sustaining reminder of where their training is taking them.

Professional Development Workshops

The TF program includes topical workshops that explain how the work world operates while also providing opportunities to develop professional and soft skills. These workshops, often given by guest speakers from industry, include topics such as time management, customer service, conflict resolution, and the Myers-Briggs personality assessment. Other programs can choose occupation-specific topics for workshops, and invite guest speakers from the industry to describe workplace examples of these topics to help students envision themselves using these skills and tools in a workplace setting. By exposing students repeatedly to professionals in the occupation for which they are training, such as through a series of guest speakers, a program can demystify and normalize these professional contacts so that students are prepared to interact with more confidence and less anxiety as they interview for and transition into new jobs.

Postgraduation Services

As documented by the Aspen Institute's Courses to Employment initiative, community college and nonprofit partners can team together to offer continuing services to and engagement with program graduates.[41] Programs most often engage graduates by asking them to share their stories with groups of new students, mentor individual students, or forward job openings and internship opportunities for students at their companies. One set of partners, Austin Community College and Capital IDEA, both in Austin,

Texas, operate an alumni association for health care program graduates. At TF, program graduates are also invited to attend periodic professional development workshops (open to current participants as well), and many program alumni choose to make modest scholarship donations in response to an annual fundraising mailing.

FIRST STEPS, OR, "WHAT CAN I DO NOW?"

While one's own experience may differ markedly from those of historically underserved students, self-reflection is nevertheless a valuable way of better understanding this stage of the transformational learning journey. Following are some introductory steps readers can take to prepare themselves to better understand and support this part of the transformation experience for students.

Personal Reflection

Take a few minutes to recall a time when you transitioned into a new and challenging role that followed a period of preparation. For some, that may be your first professional job. For others, the transition might be different, such as becoming a first-time parent or homeowner. Choose one such transition and place yourself mentally at a time and place when you were on the cusp of it. Ask yourself a few reflective questions, such as:

- Was there a moment or series of moments when you were unsure if you were cut out for this new role? What did you say to and about yourself during the time when this role felt most unnatural to you?
- When did you begin to feel more at ease in this role? What happened that led to this feeling of being more at home in your new role?

- Were there any people during this time who shepherded you, affirmed you, or made you feel like you belonged? What did these people do, specifically, that helped to build your confidence?

Experimentation

During this chapter, we described many methods or applications that instructors and advisors can deploy to assist students. They included:

- New me/old me narratives, images, and metaphors
- Direct instruction in tacit norms/code-switching
- Internships
- Service learning
- Apprenticeship programs
- Dress for success
- Early learning success
- Letter to self
- Fading support services
- Mindset intervention/assignment
- Frequent formative assessments
- Program-specific graduation rite of passage
- Peer mentors
- Success montage
- Professional development workshops with guest speakers
- Graduate services and graduate engagement

Choose one item from the list above or from your self-reflection exercise to experiment with. Your selection should be one you can implement yourself within your own role. Ideally, it is one that you believe will resonate especially well with historically underserved students to support their transition into new professional roles. Try it out, document your own observations and your student's responses. Use this introductory practice as a way to more deeply understand students' transitional journeys and how you can support them in these phases.

Interviews

You can also interview historically underserved students whom you know well to learn about experiences related to their transition into new professional careers. By interviewing at least three or four students, you will learn more about their experience and will develop your own insights into how you can support them within your role. Use versions of the questions from the self-reflection exercise above as a guide for your student interviews. After conducting the interviews, compare responses from different students to identify common themes, key variances, and ways they have been helped and that you and others at the college can adapt within your roles.

5

MOVING FORWARD

COAUTHOR BILL BROWNING recently worked closely over six months with teams of health care career education program leaders as part of a federally funded grant initiative to train low-income adults for health care careers; the programs targeted historically underserved students like those described in this book. Six of the ten program teams were led by community colleges, and the others engaged community colleges as core partners. The programs were all falling short of their employment outcome goals, and they shared an interest in determining ways to improve those outcomes. The leadership teams were guided through an exploratory process to learn about effective practices at similar programs; assess their own program's employer engagement, training, and student support practices; and identify possible changes in their practices to increase participants' success in securing health care jobs.

At the conclusion of the six-month leadership program, each team was asked to present the changes in their programs that they believed would lead to greater employment outcomes. Nearly all of the teams zeroed in on participant support services as a key to greater outcomes. While most of them already offered enhanced support services, such as career coaching, job readiness training, and end-of-program job fairs, these services were most often offered to participants as options. While the program teams made their decisions independently, many of their program change presentations were strikingly similar. Most chose to introduce a series of "job readiness" experiences and supports earlier in the students' programs of study, for example, offering career coaching prior to course enrollment, scheduling guest presentations by employers in students' initial semesters, and encouraging resume development earlier in the program. Several of them also chose to move toward requiring all students to participate in these services. Although many program leaders expressed discomfort at the prospect of limiting students' freedom of choice, one remarked that such services and experiences are "just part of the program now, like the training courses."

All ten of the teams implemented multiple changes in their program practices by the time the grant initiative was over, including all six of those led by community colleges. A few months later, a review of their program outcomes showed that the teams had raised their participants' employment outcomes by an average of nearly 100 percent compared to the previous program year.[1] These examples suggest that a holistic reassessment of program practices, with an eye toward redesigning the student experience throughout the program, holds promise for community college administrators, faculty, and advisors who want to improve program outcomes for historically underserved student groups.

STEP-BY-STEP RECOMMENDATIONS

What, then, can community college educators *do* with all of the information in this book about transformational learning? The example above provides just a glimpse of the kind of actions that an interested program administrator, department chair, faculty member, or student advisor might consider, and the kind of results that many would aspire to achieve. For those interested in putting all of the information in this book together into a plan of action, we recommend a series of six steps, described in sequence in the sections that follow. Each action step results in decisions that inform the next step. This approach is a form of *action learning*, with a sequential learning process producing immediate learning outcomes and decisions that can be applied quickly to one's work. The chapter concludes with a discussion of what change advocates can expect to experience when pioneering transformational changes within their institutions. We use Mezirow's TL framework to describe the dynamics of transformational change often encountered within an organizational change process.

Ideally, an institution-wide perspective would encourage shifting an entire college and its interwoven systems and institutional processes toward supporting the TL needs of students, but we acknowledge that such large-scale institutional change efforts would be immensely difficult to undertake, given all of the countervailing forces noted elsewhere within this book. Instead, we suggest a pilot project that targets a specific program of study or several related programs of study that attract (or need to attract) significant numbers of historically underserved students. For example, TL could be applied within health care or manufacturing technology departments. Health care employers explicitly seek a more diverse workforce to match the growing diversity of patients. Manufacturing technology employers, facing a chronic skilled labor gap and an aging workforce, need to attract younger and more diverse workers. The recommended action steps that follow are focused on department or program-level changes.

Step One: Form a Team

Program-level changes are best sponsored and led by a team of faculty and department administrators working together, ideally engaging the entire department at some level. Within most departments, there will be a range of responses from individuals, from enthusiastic advocates and early adopters of change to those who greatly prefer the comfort of traditional practices and who do not see the benefits of proposed changes.

Our first recommendation is to form a core team of three to five committed colleagues within an academic department or program of study to guide the explorations and action steps that follow. Ideally, the core team should include at least one faculty member, an advisor or student services specialist, and a program or academic department administrator, so that each of these perspectives and areas of expertise is represented in discussions and decision-making. The department head, dean, or chair—whoever is the lead decision-maker for the department—does not have to be a member of the core team, but the team needs that person to endorse and actively engage with them as a project sponsor, authorizing the team's overall initiative and approving decisions recommended by the core team during the pilot test phase. Other department colleagues and specialists from elsewhere in the college can be informed of actions and results along the way or recruited for specific supporting actions as needed.

Above all, each team member should have a sympathetic understanding of the TL journey described in this book, an aspiration to create new opportunities and improved outcomes for historically underserved student groups, and an openness to changes that can lead to better outcomes. Each of the action steps described in the following sections should engage the full team in implementing the recommended actions, reviewing what team members have learned, and making decisions. Several of the action steps will refer to previous sections of the book and will especially draw upon the findings and insights developed in the reflection activities recommended at the end of chapters 2 through 4. Having read the book and completed the reflection activities will give team members a clearer sense of students' experiences and a head start in identifying TL methods and applications to include in a pilot.

Having team members prepare in these ways for the challenge of redesigning a program of study around students' TL needs will make it easier to align perspectives and to build the trust and mutual accountability that will be needed to sustain the change effort. In order to achieve their vision and goals for improved student outcomes, the team will need to work closely together to shape the vision of what they hope to achieve and to lay out a process to test new TL methods within the department.

Step Two: Choose a Focus

The team can propose TL methods to amplify the success of an existing reform initiative, such as guided pathways or redesigned developmental education programs, or pilot them as a standalone initiative within the targeted program. Having a specific focus is critical for an effective action learning project, allowing the team to quickly apply the action steps within the specific context of the project.

Whichever you choose, make sure that the program of study or reform initiative is one that is important to the success of historically underserved students. For example, we know from research data that many historically underserved students are guided into developmental education, so any TL-informed approach within a developmental education reform initiative would match well with the students it is designed to serve. Perhaps contextualized

developmental education courses for students who plan to enroll within a specific program could become a focus for using
TL methods with targeted cohorts of students. Data also show
that historically underserved students are underenrolled in many
STEM (science, technology, engineering, and math) career education programs, which often lead to high-paying careers, so
using a TL lens within these programs, or within an entire Science and Technology department, could help increase enrollment and success rates for such students. Similarly, TL could
be a useful perspective to use for a guided pathways initiative
within a department. Groups of students who form cohorts are
already building relationships within an informal peer support
community, and the cohort-based TL methods used in programs
like Training Futures are most effective when students have begun to know and trust one another, allowing them to be more
honest without fear of being ostracized. Other options include
occupation-specific career pathway programs and apprenticeship
programs, both of which may bridge the college's noncredit and
credit divisions.

As the core team considers a specific focus for applying TL
within a department, it is likely that you will begin to identify
other areas of the institution that will need to be engaged in any
pilot program. You can identify specialists whose support will be
needed for a pilot initiative and begin to engage them to secure
their support. For example, when TF first began its coenrollment
relationship with NOVA, it needed the support of specialists
in admissions, financial aid, and student services. The sponsoring dean at NOVA invited individual specialists within each of
these departments to planning meetings where their project support roles were discussed and confirmed within an overall project

plan. As they learned how their roles contributed to the success of students enrolled in the partnership, their support strengthened over time.

There may also be opportunities to engage with contributing partners and stakeholders outside of the institution. For example, top employers of the targeted programs of study have a strong stake in the college's success and may have goals to diversify their workforce that align with your team's targeted student groups. There may also be nearby community-based nonprofits that have earned the trust of historically underserved students who could refer interested students into your program and provide additional nonacademic support services. Some of these organizations may employ career navigators who can provide ongoing holistic student support services to supplement the college's more academically oriented support services.

Step Three: Select a Target Audience

If there are already data available on the program of study you have chosen as your focus, see if it is disaggregated for various demographic groups, such as gender, age, race or ethnicity, family income status, or other characteristics that might define a target audience.[2] Select the specific underrepresented groups that you most want to attract, enroll, and serve. Your choice will be highly influenced by the project focus. For example, a STEM program focus might suggest an audience of minority and female students, typically underrepresented in STEM fields and college programs. Or you could choose to focus on low-income students from these demographic segments in particular. In developmental education, you might focus on minority and low-income students with an interest in a specific field of study who have been placed in developmental courses. A focus on low-income and minority women for manufacturing programs or low-income men for health care programs is another possibility, these groups having been historically underrepresented in those career fields and related programs of study.

Once your team has selected a target audience, review any available college and career success data, as well as their enrollment numbers compared to their representation within the region served, to establish a baseline. You may need to request disaggregated data from your college's institutional research department if such data are not available in existing reports. To establish the baseline, you should include two to three years' worth of data. This will ensure that you have a sufficient sample size and multiyear trend data, which will yield a valid baseline free from any anomalies associated with smaller sample sizes or single-year data. These baseline reports on enrollment, program retention and success, and training-related employment for your target audience will become the comparison group for a before-and-after measure of the success of your pilot program. The core team can either establish specific goals for enrollment increases, program retention and success, and employment, which can help to motivate stakeholders, or they can choose to implement a pilot program without specific goals, but with specific data results to monitor.

Step Four: Map Student Experiences

Using this book and your reflections from the previous chapters as a guide, create a map of the typical steps that any student must navigate both within the institution and within a specific program of study. For example, the map should begin with the first interaction between a prospective student and the institution, move through the application, testing, financial aid, and other onboarding processes, and continue into planning a program of study, registering for and taking classes, and accessing support services, and conclude with steps toward program completion and bridging students toward their career or further education goals. Your team's map of the student experience may look something like the example provided in figure 5.1. It may have even more detailed sequential steps within many sections, such as an "onboarding and enrollment" section that includes the college application, placement testing, financial aid, and counseling.

Use the material in chapters 2 through 4, and the results of your reflection activities following each of these chapters, to overlay the institutional processes with what you have learned about the TL experiences of historically underserved students in each of these steps. You can use this activity, combined with data reports that show when and where student success rates decline, to identify specific points throughout the student experience where these students are most likely to experience difficulties that can derail their studies and plans. This combination of using both data and a deeper understanding of student experiences to inform plans is

FIGURE 5.1

Map of students' experiences

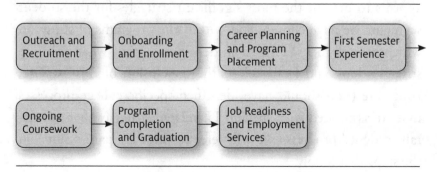

more likely to get closer to the root causes that drive the numbers and therefore more likely to result in larger gains in student success outcomes.

At what point in the institution's process and the parallel student experience do you lose students, especially those within the student segments that you have identified? Are there early-warning data indicators, or inflection points within key courses or programs of study, showing where students' academic performance takes a significant dip? Within the three TL themes (tumultuous aspects of transformation, exploring a new path forward, and re-integration), where have you observed the greatest struggles? The greatest successes? How might the TL experiences described in this book explain the struggles you have observed? This conversation may take some time, since the student experience is complex and there are many TL phases and college processes. While this discussion is oriented toward identifying struggles and barriers, it will be important for the team to also identify successful examples of student progress, in order to remind the team of the strengths and success qualities among these students. These are qualities you aim to help other students develop. Another way of relating students' TL experiences with the college processes is to take them, one at a time, and ask: What TL-related experiences and responses have we observed in each step? Which of these steps appears to present the most significant struggles for the student segments we have chosen, and within the programs of study on which we will focus? From a student perspective, what do those struggles look and feel like? At the conclusion of this exercise, your core team should have identified specific college processes that are associated with specific TL-related struggles that can derail students' progress. We will refer to these as "pain points" in the steps that follow.

Step Five: Address Pain Points

Once you have identified the most difficult challenges or pain points faced by students, the next step is to match each challenge with the TL methods of instruction and student services that would support students facing these challenges. You can begin by reviewing the book's list of TL methods at the end of chapters 2 through 4, as well as others identified by team members in their reflection activities completed earlier. For those that match up with the identified pain points, your team can also review each one to determine which of the five forms of support (as described in the introduction) each can deliver: social, practical, inspirational, reflective, and/or emotional (SPIRE). The purpose behind this activity is to prompt you to think about the forms of support students need and how you plan to provide them. Also, in putting together the implementation of these methods and including all the nitty-gritty details, you may be able to design them to provide multiple forms of support rather than just one. By analyzing proposed methods using SPIRE, you will make each method more intentionally focused on supporting students along their transformational journey.

As an example, see table 5.1 for all of the potential applications mentioned in this book, each application matched with the aspects of transformation it is primarily designed to address and the forms of support it provides.

One lesson we have learned in our conversations with TF faculty and staff is that the TL learning and support methods that seem most helpful are those that address multiple forms of support. Choose a series of specific TL activities, including some mix of new instructional methods and student support services, that can address the most significant pain points you identified, and that offer a variety of the forms of support that they may need.

TABLE 5.1

Potential Transformational Learning applications and the forms of support they provide

APPLICATION	FORM OF SUPPORT
Tumultuous Aspects of Transformation	
Disorienting Dilemma	
• Vision-Reality exercise	practical, inspirational
• "Letting Go" balloon exercise	inspirational, emotional
• Comfort/Discomfort Zone ("Inner Pig")	inspirational
Self-Examination with Intense Emotions	
• Individualized counseling	emotional
• Bell-ringing celebration ritual	inspirational
• Life philosophy presentation	practical, reflective
• Graduate panel discussion	inspirational, emotional
Critical Self-Assessment	
• Quote conversations	inspirational, reflective
• Structured critical thinking exercises	practical, reflective
Recognition That Others Have Been There	
• Structured socializing	social
• Forums and support groups	social, emotional
• Sharing stories	practical, inspirational, emotional
Exploring the Path Forward	
Exploring Options	
• Employer engagement	social, practical
• Collaborating with stakeholders	practical, inspirational
• Holistic advising	practical, inspirational, emotional
Making a Plan	
• Performance review meetings	practical, reflective
• Career pathway planning	practical, inspirational
• Getting and Keeping a Job (GKJ)	social, practical
Acquiring Needed Knowledge and Skills	
• Immersion in context of practice	social, practical
• Work-based simulations	practical
• Create an immersive environment	social

Reintegration

Trying On New Roles
- Teaching code-switching — social, practical
- Internships — social, practical
- Service/Community-based learning — social, practical, reflective
- Dress for success — practical, inspirational

Building Competence and Self-Confidence
- Early learning success — inspirational
- Letter to self — inspirational
- Peer mentoring — inspirational, emotional
- Fading supports — practical, inspirational
- Mindsets — practical, inspirational
- Formative assessments — practical, inspirational

Reintegration into One's Life
- Success Montage — inspirational
- Professional development workshops — social, practical, inspirational
- Postgraduation services — social, practical

For each of the applications you choose to implement, consider at what level it would be best to offer it (see table 5.2). The various levels at which support can be offered are:

- In a particular course
- In multiple or all program courses
- Through programmatic activities outside of the classroom
- Through programmatic or institutional resources made available to students
- Through the overall design of the program

The applications listed above are not intended to represent an all-encompassing list of structural supports suitable for all institutions and their respective academic programs. We culled this list

TABLE 5.2

Transformational Learning applications and the levels at which support can be provided

APPLICATION	LEVEL
Tumultuous Aspects of Transformation	
Disorienting Dilemma	
- Vision-Reality exercise	single course
- "Letting Go" balloon exercise	single course; activities
- Comfort/Discomfort Zone ("Inner Pig")	single course
Self-Examination with Intense Emotions	
- Individualized counseling	program resources
- Bell-ringing celebration ritual	activities
- Life philosophy presentation	activities
- Graduate panel discussion	activities
Critical Self-Assessment	
- Quote conversations	multiple courses
- Structured critical thinking exercises	multiple courses
Recognition That Others Have Been There	
- Structured socializing	program design
- Forums and support groups	program design
- Sharing stories	activities
Exploring the Path Forward	
Exploring Options	
- Employer engagement	multiple courses; activities; program design
- Collaborating with stakeholders	program design
- Holistic advising	program resources; program design
Making a Plan	
- Performance review meetings	multiple courses; activities; program design
- Career pathway planning	multiple courses; program design
- Getting and Keeping a Job (GKJ)	multiple courses; activities
Acquiring Needed Knowledge and Skills	
- Immersion in context of practice	multiple courses
- Work-based simulations	multiple courses
- Create an immersive environment	multiple courses; activities

Reintegration	
Trying On New Roles	
- Teaching code-switching	multiple courses
- Internships	multiple courses; program design
- Service/Community-based learning	multiple courses; program design
- Dress for success	multiple courses; program design
Building Competence and Self-Confidence	
- Early learning success	multiple courses
- Letter to self	multiple courses; activities
- Peer mentoring	multiple courses; program design
- Fading supports	multiple courses
- Mindsets	multiple courses
- Formative assessments	multiple courses
Reintegration into One's Life	
- Success Montage	activities
- Professional development workshops	activities; program resources
- Postgraduation services	program resources

simply from the examples provided in this book. Some of them may seem to overlap with each other, and there may be more or better applications suitable for your particular program. Nevertheless, the structure we recommend is to:

1. consider the needs of historically underserved students presented in this chapter;
2. design applications that provide appropriate forms of support for these specific needs; and
3. decide on the most appropriate level at which to include each application.

Step Six: Test and Assess

Your team has made decisions and gathered the information needed to implement a live-action pilot project to test your proposed changes with actual students. By this point, the team should have assembled the following information that can be written into a summary report, which then can be readily converted into a project plan:

- *Project Team*: In addition to the core team, your work to date should also include identification of other contributors to a pilot effort, including colleagues within your department and outside of the department. Hopefully, you have engaged each of these additional contributors and attracted their interest in participating or confirmed their participation in a pilot.
- *Area of Focus*: You have chosen an area of focus that helps to define the scope of your pilot project. For example, you may have chosen to focus on a stand-alone program within one academic department or one or more related programs of study. Alternatively, you have chosen a department or program of study and an existing reform project, such as guided pathways or developmental education, in order to amplify success rates using TL methods within the chosen program of study or department.
- *Targeted Underserved Student Audience*: You have selected specific groups of historically underserved students as the primary focus of your pilot project. While your pilot may also include and benefit other students, your efforts will highlight the impact on specific student groups who are likely to be experiencing the challenges associated with TL; this may include minorities, low-income households, and/ or first-generation college students. You have also gathered baseline data for these targeted student groups, such as enrollment, retention, completion, and employment success rates within the targeted programs of study.

- *Pain Point Map*: You have mapped out the student experience from outreach to completion and employment, and you identified specific pain points within the student experience where the student groups you have looked at have often struggled or discontinued their progress altogether. These pain points identify specific areas where there is a need for new practices or methods that will enable students to address these areas of difficulty within a transformational change process.
- *Transformational Learning Methods to Test*: For each of the pain points, your team has identified specific TL methods to help students navigate each area of difficulty. These may include TL instructional methods, support services, or other activities that are designed to help students navigate and address these difficult moments of personal change so that they become transformational learning experiences rather than barriers that block or disrupt their progress.

This live testing phase will involve more detailed development of the TL methods you have chosen, careful observations and adjustments during implementation of these new methods, and a pilot duration of at least two academic terms. We recommend that you develop a project plan so that all contributors to the pilot project know their roles and how their contributions fit into the overall design of the pilot, know the timeline for taking specific actions, and know what kinds of measures will be used to assess success rates. The team should assemble at specific points during the pilot to assess progress, difficulties encountered, and needed adjustments to the plans. For example, during the initial years when NOVA and TF jointly ran their coenrollment program, contributors from both organizations gathered to develop a joint project plan for the program. Each term, the plan was sharpened to improve the delivery process and outcomes, and eventually the plan listed a sequence of twenty-eight action steps, with individual accountabilities for each one, that led to achievement of four primary program outcomes.[3]

In developing a pilot plan, the team can identify formative assessments or indicators during the implementation that can help your team determine whether your TL interventions are helping the targeted student groups, and to give you quick feedback for making adjustments. Be sure to document plans, assessments, and adjustments during the pilot project so that any future implementation can build upon what was learned during the pilot. After the second term of the pilot, compare the results achieved with the baseline measures gathered earlier to determine if the results have changed for the targeted student groups. Depending on the results, the team may decide to continue the pilot on a modest scale and continue refining the approach, to begin expanding the pilot if results show substantial promise, or to begin the process anew if the effort does not show potential for improved student outcomes.

WHAT TO EXPECT DURING A TRANSFORMATIONAL LEARNING JOURNEY FOR COMMUNITY COLLEGE EDUCATORS

Many reforms have tested modest departures from established norms, often with limited results for historically underserved students. The action steps described in this chapter, however, are likely to result in more systematic changes, allowing student experiences to guide the changes in multiple overlapping processes and systems. For community college professionals, this level of systemic change is likely to be truly transformational, requiring a significant shift in perspective about the institution or department and how it supports students, along with a readiness to overhaul core processes including instruction, student support, and other administrative steps that students must complete. In other words, the journey by teams of faculty and staff leaders to explore and pilot TL methods in community colleges is likely to follow a process of transformation similar to the one described for students throughout this book. The TL journey, after all, is a universal human experience. Nobody is immune to the challenges of it, certainly not community college faculty and staff seeking to change the ways they have taught or advised students, working with colleagues similarly acculturated to the taken-for-granted academic process of delivering technical knowledge, and working within the institutional policies that have evolved to reinforce this model. In this section, we offer a preview of some of the dynamics that teams may expect to experience during the process of leading transformational changes.

The journey, for those who accept a call to action, is personal, examining one's own perspective about student learning and about instructional and advising practices in order to support students who need *you* to change in order for them to have a better chance at success. It is relational, positively affecting one's relationships with peers who join in, and causing stress and possible conflict with those who want to stick with traditional practices. And it is institutional, challenging established organizational culture and processes that some will fight to defend.

Shift your perspective to see the institution and its processes through the eyes of the students you have chosen to serve. This book has provided many examples of how college processes meant to help students may unintentionally create barriers that block success, especially for historically underserved students. The reflection activities in chapters 2 through 4 were designed to deepen the reader's understanding of the student experience of profound personal change. It is easy and natural to allow your professional perspective to distance you from students' experiences. In order to effectively redesign the college experience to remove barriers and support students undergoing change, one must take on the students' perspective to better understand the often unseen and easy-to-forget effects of their transformational learning.

Use admission of uncomfortable failures to energize change. For a community college professional who believes in the mission of education with the potential to change lives for the better, confronting low completion success rates for historically underserved student groups should be uncomfortable. Confronting the system's failure of a major group of students should be disorienting, leading to questions that can quickly bump up against established norms. An honest acknowledgement of failure can also provide a motivational springboard for groups of colleagues within a program of study who want to do more to attract, teach, and graduate more students who are better equipped to succeed in new career fields. By creating a disequilibrium that leads to questioning traditional thinking about how a department teaches and supports students, this disorienting dilemma opens up a space and moment in time to consider systematic changes, and it makes possible the development of a new perspective about what is possible.

Coauthor Browning recently documented three case studies of high performing health care training programs that yielded an interesting pattern. None of the three program examples had been high performing for very long. In each case, program leaders had encountered modestly disappointing program results over the previous several years; refusing to settle for comfortable mediocrity, they each embarked on a change process that took their teams out of their comfort zones to operate their health care training programs in significantly different ways than before. The technical solutions chosen by the three were all very different, but the process of experiencing a disorienting disappointment that energized new momentum for significant changes in their program or institutional practices was similar. After successfully navigating program changes, all of these cases documented rising student completion and employment outcomes in their programs. While the experience of honestly confronting disappointments can be intensely uncomfortable, the questions that arise from them can remove blinders limiting our vision about what is possible and lead to a new and empowering vision of success and how to achieve it.

Wrestle as a group with the emotional reactions to departmental failures or disappointments. Having honest discussions about the departmental shortcomings that contribute to poor results, including low enrollment rates, can be explosive and dredge up fears among colleagues that must be heard and responded to. When encountering this difficult phase, there is a temptation to downplay the scale of inquiry and associated changes, or to quietly file initial data studies or reports into the archives and move on with business as usual. Continuing with what the community college reform organization Achieving the Dream calls "courageous conversations" about uncomfortable data requires honesty and trust among key investigative leaders within the department in order to persist with the inquiry.[4]

Question the value of traditional norms and processes. An essential part of an honest departmental self-evaluation is to allow and facilitate conversations about assumptions that may not been questioned before. Like people, organizations accumulate habits, cultural values, and worldviews, and some of these may have outlived their usefulness. Asking difficult questions may cause stress with colleagues who prefer the comfort of traditional process over the risks of change. These questions might help get to the heart of diagnosing the student pain points discussed above. For example, how is it possible that one standardized test can determine if a student is "college-ready," regardless of whether the student intends to take general education courses and transfer to an elite university or wants to study to be an auto technician? Might students build basic skills more quickly and successfully if they learn them within their technical studies coursework and as they are applied within the field of study, rather than learning them sequentially before a college program of study and stripped of the usefulness of how they are applied? Are work-based learning program models like apprenticeships and internships that align competency-based technical instruction with structured on-the-job learning a better way of preparing students for new careers than classroom-only instruction? Do colleges need to create and directly operate all programs and services on their own, or might it be more affordable and effective to acquire some new capacities through strategic partnerships?

At the department level, one overarching question asked throughout this book is about the learning process that lies at the core of a program of study. If many students are experiencing a difficult process of personal change, why do the course curricula and instructional strategies within the program of study assume that students need only technical knowledge and skills? Asking and addressing fundamental questions such as this about previously accepted standards and practices are difficult for some professionals to even consider. However, such questions create an interest in exploring alternatives that might not otherwise be considered.

Be prepared to encounter moments of truth when you will be tested. New initiatives that involve changes in previous processes, cultural practices, and people's jobs need to carefully balance a hard-nosed, results-driven plan with careful listening to and support for stakeholders affected by the changes. Stakeholders may accurately identify risks that necessitate changes in plans, and they may have emotional reactions that call for dialogue. Not all stakeholders will come around in support of the plan, and some of their voices, either individually or collectively, may have considerable influence to delay or even block elements of the plan. In those situations, ongoing conflicts that are not resolvable at the project management level may need to be escalated to the department head or even executive sponsor to address.

For larger risks associated with changes, there may be moments of truth that can make or break a systemic reform initiative or pilot project. For example, when NOVA's leaders were preparing for reaccreditation several years ago, the issue of the faculty credentials of TF instructors (who had previously been reviewed, and who were considered qualified NOVA adjunct faculty) was raised and discussed at an executive level. Several of the TF faculty members had excellent instructional records and additional post-secondary training in their fields, but did not possess eighteen graduate credit hours in their specific teaching disciplines. These faculty therefore had to demonstrate their qualifications using alternative methods. Alternative credentialing was allowed in some cases under regional accreditation standards, but NOVA's chief academic officer pointed out that multiple uses of alternative faculty credentialing could invite the risk of receiving a warning from accreditation reviewers. NOVA's president responded that the partnership would probably not survive if NOVA insisted on such rigid qualifications for successful TF instructors. Given the consequences to the partnership, it was agreed that taking on this modest risk in the accreditation process was acceptable, and the resulting accreditation assessment went well.

Be prepared to champion and advise scaling across other departments if the pilot is successful. At some point, after repeating and adjusting new practices at the program level, what was once new, uncertain, and uncomfortable will feel more comfortable and more accepted by stakeholders within the pilot project team. As new practices are perfected and student results observed in the pilot initiative, the project team can become champions inside the institution who can show the way for other programs within their own or other departments to adopt these practices. In order for practices to be effectively transmitted and adapted across multiple departments or programs, the pilot initiative must be carefully documented, and the pilot team must be able to provide others with tools such as accountability charts, process maps, project plans, lesson plans, and assessment measures.

However, this challenge of navigating transformational change calls for more than just technical information and solutions. Institutions like community colleges are made up of people who come to work every day with a swirling mix of fears and doubts, strengths and hopes. The project team within the sponsoring department will likely also have experienced this mix of reactions as they pioneered their program's changes. Stories of their own personal learning journeys can be powerful testimonies to the TL process within the organization. Like the TF program graduates who return to share their experiences with new cohorts of train-ees, the pilot team members can share with interested colleagues their personal stories of doubt and anxiety about taking a per-sonal leap into the unknown, and should also share the problems that they encountered and had to address along the way. This pro-cess calls to mind the keynote speaker at a TF graduation a num-ber of years ago, Julie Portman, a noted playwright, actor, and storyteller. In her remarks to the graduating participants, she said:

> When I visited Training Futures and listened to a panel of gradu-ates counseling new trainees, I felt like I was at a Mountain Climb-ing Institute. When climbers scale new heights, they leave behind marks for those who come after them . . . Stories like these build community. That's what we're missing so often today because we stopped listening to each other's stories. . . . I need to hear your stories. They help me, help us all. Your stories change the world.

APPENDIX

Case Study: NOVA–Training Futures Partnership

THROUGHOUT THE BOOK, we have included student quotes and vignettes from the Training Futures program. For readers who are curious to learn more about the program, this appendix describes the program, the transformational learning model that underpins the program's design, and the evolving partnership between Training Futures and Northern Virginia Community College (NOVA).

Training Futures is a workforce development program operated by a regional social services organization called Northern Virginia Family Service (NVFS). Coauthor Bill Browning served as the program manager overseeing Training Futures (along with one other workforce development program) for five years, from 2001–06, and led the initial partnership phase with NOVA during these years. NOVA is a large community college with annual credit enrollments of approximately 70,000 students and six campuses located in the northern Virginia suburbs of Washington, DC. From 2006–13, he worked within NOVA's workforce development division and as special assistant to the president, and he served in an ongoing advisory role to assist college administrators in managing the partnership with Training Futures. Browning collected all of the participant quotes and stories that are included in this book between 2001 and 2013. Since 2013, the alliance between the two organizations has continued to evolve, and has taken on a less formal shape during the two years preceding the publication of this book.

AN OVERVIEW OF THE TRAINING FUTURES PROGRAM

Training Futures was founded in 1996 by two experienced nonprofit leaders, Susan Craver and Marla Burton, who worked together in a workforce development program in Washington, DC. Craver led the program and organization as the executive director; Burton was a business volunteer in the program and worked as the executive director at a nearby national nonprofit organization. They wanted to offer a similar program in their home community of Northern Virginia, just across the Potomac River from the nation's capital. They formed an alliance with leaders of NVFS, which had identified a need for a new job training program in the region. Training Futures has been a program of NVFS throughout its history.

The two cofounders divided management duties in leading daily program operations, and each also taught courses within the program from its 1996 launch until they both retired in 2013. The program enrolled unemployed and low-wage workers who lacked the basic computer skills needed to break free from dead-end retail and service jobs and launch new careers in a professional office environment. To be accepted into the program, applicants had to score at a sixth-grade level or higher on a basic English and math skills test, and demonstrate motivation to persist during an interview. The three or four program staff members at each program site served as instructional faculty teaching specific course material that matched their expertise.[1] Each also handled the supervision and advising of approximately ten participants.

While there were frequent changes in the program curriculum, during most of the time frame covered within this book Training Futures was a twenty-five-week training program held every weekday from nine a.m. to two p.m., totaling over 500 hours of classroom time. The program curriculum was designed to prepare participants for a variety of entry-level office administrative jobs, such as receptionist, program assistant, file clerk, and data entry clerk. Each cohort enrolled a total of thirty to forty-five participants, divided into fifteen-person sections that rotated between different course modules during each day, similar to the format used by many college cohort programs. The curriculum included instructional modules on keyboarding (touch-typing skills); the Microsoft Office software suite of Word, Excel, PowerPoint, and Access; filing and records management; customer service; and a series of professional development topics such as time management, stress management, and the like. In 2006, Training Futures added specialized curriculum modules such as the medical terminology needed for fast-growing medical office and hospital administrative jobs, which lengthened the skill-building portion of the program from fourteen to seventeen weeks. After completing the skill-building segment of the program, participants were placed into three-week internship positions with employer-partners. The final five weeks of the program, called Getting and Keeping a Job, prepared students for job searching and for a successful transition into a new professional career field.

TRAINING FUTURES' TRANSFORMATIONAL LEARNING PROGRAM MODEL

From its inception, Training Futures was envisioned by its co-founders as a vehicle for participants to engage in the deep personal change needed to successfully launch a new career. This transformational change approach is called Imaginal Education.[2] Based on the work of Kenneth Boulding, imaginal education was first pioneered by the Institute for Cultural Affairs in the 1970s as a response to the problem of job training program graduates who did not succeed in adapting to their professional environments and too often lost their new jobs shortly after being hired. Similar in many ways to Mezirow's transformational learning model, imaginal education holds that people operate from images of themselves and their worlds, and that these deeply embedded images guide behavior in many unseen ways. This approach also acknowledges that one's images can change, and the program provides constant opportunities in every aspect of the program experience for participants to evaluate and change their operating images (that is, the internalized pictures of ourselves and our place in the world that influence our decisions and behaviors) to more closely resemble the successful professionals that they are learning to become. When one's images shift, then new behaviors for new environments (such as college and a professional workplace) can take root and be sustained over time.[3]

Program staff and volunteers have witnessed the consistent effort and difficult emotional journey required to successfully navigate transformational change, and they have developed a profound respect for the courage that it takes for participants to undergo this process and stick with it through all of the challenges. These eyewitness encounters help to reinforce the strengths-based approach that is another feature of the imaginal education model. As a result, what many participants experience (that is, how they are treated throughout the program by the entire network of professionals and volunteers they encounter) reinforces their aspiration to change and helps to sustain them through the rough patches.

What does imaginal education look like in practice? As noted in the Introduction, the Training Futures program design was unencumbered by the constraints of a traditional college campus environment, culture, and practices. In fact, the program's site is intentionally located within a business district, so that participants are exposed to business culture just by being there. For colleges or college programs, the interwoven practices used at Training Futures (many of which have been described in previous chapters) represent a fresh design based on principles of transformational learning and built around the needs of historically underserved students who embark on a semester-long journey of transformation in order to become successful professionals. Some of the design features include:

- *Immersion into the culture of the professional workplace*, such as timesheets and progressive discipline for being late (including potential termination), a dress code, supervisors and performance reviews, and project-based learning assignments that resemble common workplace tasks within the targeted entry-level occupations.
- *Intentional support community of diverse peers* in each cohort who provide ongoing peer-to-peer support and encouragement, including program graduates who return to share their stories of struggle and success.
- *Direct exposure to the workplace and professionals*, including guest presentations by employers, computer coaching and email practice with business volunteers, site visits to employer locations, and a three-week internship placement.
- *Quote conversations at the start of each course module*, happening several times daily to bring to the surface and assess one's underlying self-images and self-talk, totaling over

300 quote conversations through which participants can consciously choose how to update their operating images.

- *Personalized support services*, including regularly scheduled consultations with a faculty advisor, access to a professional counselor or social worker, and volunteer coaches and tutors as needed.

THE EVOLVING TRAINING FUTURES–NOVA PARTNERSHIP

The partnership between Training Futures and Northern Virginia Community College began in 2002, when a survey of Training Futures program graduates showed that nearly 90 percent of them were interested in college, but only 14 percent had taken any college courses since completing Training Futures. With multiple campuses throughout the Northern Virginia region, NOVA was the natural choice for a college partner. In his role as program manager, Browning made several initial attempts to connect with college administrators at the two closest campuses, but initial overtures failed to identify a champion willing to invest time in exploring a partnership. However, Jenny Graves, a dean of the Business Studies department at NOVA's Alexandria, Virginia, campus took an interest, visited the program, and met the staff and students. Seeing how closely matched the computer skills training was to similar courses in her department, she chose to lead a faculty effort to evaluate the program's computer training curriculum modules for potential prior learning credit at NOVA. The Training Futures team also agreed to add a one-credit "college success skills" course to the program's curriculum, giving successful program graduates a total of seven credits.

Also in 2002, Dr. Robert Templin Jr. became president at NOVA. He was interested in identifying ways to better serve underrepresented members of the Northern Virginia community, especially recent immigrant families, a sector that had grown rapidly to become approximately 25 percent of the region's population. President Templin signaled his support for the proposed partnership with Training Futures when he arrived unannounced to attend the faculty meeting held to consider the curriculum review team's recommendation to award six college credits at NOVA for Training Futures participants who successfully completed the computer skills training courses within the curriculum. When asked at the meeting to share his perspective, President Templin spoke about the need for the college to create community-based partnerships to jointly serve low-income students in more holistic ways. The committee voted to approve the prior learning credits at Training Futures.

Shortly after the committee's approval, President Templin spoke at a Training Futures graduation event, and announced the partnership to a group of surprised program graduates who were unaware of the faculty course review process.[4] "By graduating from Training Futures, you've taken the first step towards the American dream of educational opportunity, economic opportunity, and home ownership. . . . You are now admitted to NOVA, and not only that, by completing Training Futures you've earned seven NOVA college credits!" He said later that he expected modest positive response to the news. Instead, there were audible gasps from surprised graduates, followed by a long standing ovation, and then many graduates clutched their new transcripts closely to their chests with expressions of pride and joy that surprised him.

In 2006, NOVA's Jenny Graves and the Training Futures program team decided to deepen the partnership, and the entire more than 500-hour curriculum was reviewed to identify which courses—in addition to the two computer courses—might be aligned with existing NOVA courses. After a few adjustments in the Training Futures courses, the group identified a total of seventeen credit hours of matching coursework. These courses comprised most of the credits needed to earn NOVA's Business Information Technology certificate.

By leveraging financial aid, for which nearly all of Training Futures' low-income students were eligible, and qualifying Training Futures instructors as adjunct college faculty, the two partners began to coenroll newly accepted students at both Training Futures and NOVA. Rather than earning seven prior learning credits as before, students could earn up to seventeen credits, with a college credential—NOVA's Business Information Technology certificate—within reach if the student completed just a couple more NOVA courses after finishing at Training Futures. When President Templin was briefed about this new coenrollment partnership, his main concern was for the integrity of the program's transformational learning practices, which he referred to as Training Futures' "special sauce." The only change in this regard was that the Training Futures program team now added a new emphasis on transformational learning activities to build images of college success, in addition to its prior focus exclusively on employment success.

TRAINING FUTURES' PROGRAM RESULTS

In 2007, the Training Futures–NOVA partnership was one of six community college–workforce program partnerships selected by the Aspen Institute for a three-year demonstration project, called Courses to Employment.[5] In 2011, the Aspen Institute published a data study on the Training Futures–NOVA partnership that describes the student demographics and program results over three years (2007–10), as shown in the tables A.1 and A.2.[6]

TABLE A.1
Training Futures–NOVA partnership

Training Futures Student Profile (253 total enrolled students)	
Age	median age: 38 range: 20 to over 50
Gender	75% female; 25% male
Ethnicity	26.1% Middle Eastern 21.3% African American 20.2% Asian 14.6% Hispanic 9.5% Caucasian 7.5% African 0.8% Multiethnic
Native Language/ English Levels	64% non-native English speakers minimum English at entry: 6th-grade level
Employment Status at Enrollment	51% employed; 49% unemployed
Household Income and Prior Wages	79% have household income under 125% of poverty level prior average wage: $10.29 per hour

TABLE A.2
Training Futures program outcomes

Training Futures Program Outcomes (253 total enrolled students)	
Successful Program Completion	94%
NOVA College Credits Earned	84% earned NOVA college credits median: 17 credits earned
New Training-Related Employment Within Six Months of Program Completion	84%
Wage Gain	Average wage with new job: $13.31 per hour 29% average wage increase over prior earnings
College Continuation at NOVA (following Training Futures Program Completion)	18% prior to final cohort during the three-year study 46% in final cohort that had ongoing access to a college advisor during the program

Through the coenrollment partnership with Training Futures, NOVA enrolled nearly 100 historically underserved students per year who would have been unlikely to enroll at the college on their own. Partly by leveraging the transformational learning methods of Training Futures, over 80 percent of students successfully completed an equivalent of seventeen college credits during the five-month program. Within a few months, over 80 percent of program completers secured new professional-track jobs, lifting their household earnings by an average of 29 percent. Multiple surveys of program graduates showed that many of them continued to advance in their careers, suggesting a continued ability to learn and adapt to new professional challenges and environments over time.

These success rates for Training Futures participants contrast sharply with what similar students experience at community colleges. The student profile outlined on the first table includes subgroups that generally produce low success rates at college, especially the "triple nontraditional" combination represented by the majority of Training Futures students, who are nonwhite, speak intermediate-level English as a second language, and who come from low-income households. Instead of floundering at the start of their college studies, at Training Futures these students thrive, succeed in the initial program at high rates, and go on to launch successful new careers at equally high success rates. What's the difference? As we saw from the NOVA faculty team review and alignment process described above, the "traditional" course curriculum, as defined by material covered within course syllabi, is the same in both places. It is hard to avoid concluding that the primary difference is the transformational learning curriculum built into every element of the Training Futures program and experienced by participants multiple times every weekday for twenty-five weeks.

In reflecting on a successful career launch, Training Futures program graduates most often highlight elements of the program's transformational change process, such as the support community of peers, or the staff's affirmation and faith in their abilities. When program graduates debrief their overall experience with program staff, one remark heard regularly was "you saw potential in me that I couldn't see for myself." The Training Futures program described in this appendix shows what is possible when program administrators and faculty see potential rather than only risks with historically underserved students, and when they provide support and guidance for those students to undertake a learning journey of deep personal change.

NOTES

INTRODUCTION

1. Jack Mezirow, Gordon G. Darkenwald, and Alan Boyd Knox, *Last Gamble on Education* (Washington, DC: American Adult Education Association, 1975), 1.

2. Although it is possible to enjoy a life-sustaining standard of living without a college degree, the odds of doing so are extremely low. See Ron Haskins, Harry Holzer, and Robert Lerman, *Promoting Economic Mobility by Increasing Postsecondary Education* (Washington, DC: Brookings Institution, 2009), https://www.brookings.edu/research/promoting-economic-mobility-by-increasing-postsecondary-education/.

3. The academic literature more commonly uses the term "transformative learning" rather than "transformational learning." However, the terms are interchangeable; we will use the latter term in this book.

4. We borrow this term from Dowd and Bensimon and use it rather than *minority* to highlight the fact that minority status is not a natural or inevitable occurrence; rather, it is placed on certain groups through the beliefs and social processes enacted by other groups. There are certainly many community colleges serving areas in which the racially minoritized students are in fact the majority. See Alicia C. Dowd and Estela Mara Bensimon, *Engaging the "Race Question": Accountability and Equity in US Higher Education* (New York: Teachers College Press, 2015), 8.

5. We want to emphasize that while historically underserved students enroll in higher education with multiple challenges compared to the historically served students, many of them also bring a powerful determination to change their lives through education, wisdom, and resilience gained through hard-earned experience, and they often convey a sense of deep gratitude for any support or guidance offered by faculty, advisors, or administrators.

6. Dowd and Bensimon, *Engaging the Race Question*, 15.

7. We use the Training Futures nonprofit training program and its partnership with Northern Virginia Community College throughout this book as an example of a program that explicitly sought to support students in their transformational changes while in school. More information on TF is provided later in this chapter and in the appendix.

8. Doug Shapiro et al., *Completing College: A National View of Student Completion Rates —Fall 2011 Cohort*, Signature Report No. 14 (Herndon, VA: National

Student Clearinghouse Research Center, 2017), https://nscresearchcenter.org
/signaturereport14/.

9. Much of the following narrative about the history of the community college system
is drawn from Joshua Wyner, *Community College 3.0: What's Next for the Student
Success Agenda?* (North Carolina: Dallas Herring Lecture, November 14, 2016).

10. Thomas D. Snyder, Cristobal de Brey, and Sally A. Dillow, *Digest of Education Statistics 2016* (NCES 2017-094), National Center for Education Statistics, Institute
of Education Sciences, United States Department of Education (2018), https://nces
.ed.gov/pubs2017/2017094.pdf.

11. Thomas D. Snyder, Cristobal de Brey, and Sally A. Dillow, *Digest of Education Statistics 2015* (NCES 2106-014), National Center for Education Statistics, Institute
of Education Sciences, United States Department of Education (2016), https://nces
.ed.gov/pubs2016/2016014.pdf.

12. American Association of Community Colleges, "Fast Facts" (Washington, DC:
American Association of Community Colleges, 2018), https://www.aacc.nche.edu
/research-trends/fast-facts/. Community college continuing education divisions offer an increasing array of occupational training programs for students to acquire
nondegree credentials needed for middle-skill jobs, such as industry-recognized
certifications, occupational licensing, and apprenticeships.

13. Another term commonly used is *pre-curriculum courses.* These courses teach prerequisite skills, usually in math, writing, and reading, to prepare students for the
curriculum-level courses. One of their main disadvantages, however, is that they
cannot be credited toward the student's degree or other credential.

14. Thomas R. Bailey, *Challenge and Opportunity: Rethinking the Role and Function of
Developmental Education in Community College* (New York: Community College Research Center, 2009), 11–30, https://ccrc.tc.columbia.edu/publications/challenge
-and-opportunity.html.

15. Thomas R. Bailey and Sung-Woo Cho, *Developmental Education in Community
Colleges* (New York: Community College Research Center, 2010), https://ccrc.tc
.columbia.edu/publications/developmental-education-in-community-colleges.html.
We recognize that 28+30+10=68, and thus there remained 32% of students who
completed the coursework. We assume the difference (31% instead of 32%) is due
to rounding.

16. Many colleges are now experimenting with new solutions for this problem of academically unprepared students, such as cocurricular, rather than pre-curriculum,
coursework.

17. Although we talk of TF in the present tense, our description is based solely on the
time period 2003–13. The program is continually evolving, so elements of the program have changed since then, as have the specifics of its partnership with Northern Virginia Community College.

18. Training Futures conducted formal surveys of its program graduates in 2003,
2006, and 2010, from which these composite results were taken. While the survey
questions changed slightly over the years, the results were remarkably consistent

in showing high levels of employment retention, career advancement, earnings growth, and access to employment benefits.

19. Maureen Conway, Amy Blair, and Matt Helmer, *Courses to Employment: Partnering to Create Paths to Education and Careers* (Washington, DC: Aspen Institute, 2012), https://assets.aspeninstitute.org/content/uploads/files/content/docs/pubs/C2E.pdf.

20. Jack Mezirow and Associates, *Learning as Transformation: Critical Perspectives on a Theory in Progress* (San Francisco: Jossey-Bass Publishers, 2000), 22.

CHAPTER 1

1. Jack Mezirow and associates, *Learning as Transformation: Critical Perspectives on a Theory in Progress* (San Francisco: Jossey-Bass, 2000), 6.

2. For the most thorough presentation of his theory, see Jack Mezirow, *Transformative Dimensions of Adult Learning* (San Francisco: Jossey-Bass, 1991). For a more concise version, we particularly like Jack Mezirow, *Learning to Think Like an Adult* (San Francisco: Jossey-Bass, 2000), 3–33.

3. Mezirow later changed his terminology from *meaning perspectives* to *frames of reference*. For a history of the development of Mezirow's theory, see Andrew Kitchenham, "The Evolution of John Mezirow's Transformative Learning Theory," *Journal of Transformative Education* 6, no. 2 (April 2008): 104–23, doi:10.1177/1541344608322678. To avoid confusion, in this book we are using Mezirow's original term.

4. Mezirow described several types of meaning perspectives that everyone has, three of which are particularly relevant for our discussion here. One type of meaning perspective is sociolinguistic; this includes such things as one's cultural canon, ideologies, and social norms. Second, there are psychological meaning perspectives, which include one's self-concept, personality traits, personality types, emotional response patterns, and "repressed parental prohibitions that continue to dictate ways of feeling and acting in adulthood." Third, there are epistemic meaning perspectives, which include one's learning styles, sensory preferences, and whether one tends to focus on wholes or parts, and on the concrete or the abstract. The other types of meaning perspectives Mezirow describes are: moral-ethical, philosophical, and aesthetic. See Mezirow, *Learning as Transformation*, 16–17.

5. Mezirow, *Transformative Dimensions of Adult Learning*, 4–5.

6. Mezirow, *Learning as Transformation*, 16.

7. Mezirow, *Transformative Dimensions of Adult Learning*.

8. See Ken Bain, *What the Best College Teachers Do* (Cambridge, MA: Harvard University Press, 2011) for some illustrative examples of how this phenomenon plays out in a college classroom.

9. There is actually a subtle distinction between "transformative learning" and "perspective transformation," but this distinction is not necessary for our purposes here. For more information, see Chad D. Hoggan, "Transformative Learning as a Metatheory: Definition, Criteria, and Typology," *Adult Education Quarterly* 66, no. 1 (November 2015): 57–75, doi:10.1177/0741713615611216.

10. Hoggan, "Transformative Learning as a Metatheory," 71.

11. Edward W. Taylor, Patricia Cranton, and Associates, *The Handbook of Transformative Learning: Theory, Research, and Practice* (San Francisco: Jossey-Bass, 2012).

12. This analysis is based on Chad D. Hoggan, "A Typology of Transformation: Reviewing the Transformative Learning Literature," *Studies in the Education of Adults* 48, no. 1 (May 2016): 65–82, doi:10.1080/02660830.2016.1155849.

13. Mary Anderson, Jane Goodman, and Nancy Schlossberg, *Counseling Adults in Transition: Linking Schlossberg's Theory with Practice in a Diverse World* (New York: Springer Publishing Company, 2011).

14. Albert Bandura, "Self-Efficacy: Toward a Unifying Theory of Behavioral Change," *Psychological Review* 84, no. 2 (1977): 191–215, doi:10.1037/0033-295X.84.2.191.

15. American Psychological Association, *The Road to Resilience* (Washington, DC: American Psychological Association, 2018), http://www.apa.org/helpcenter/road-resilience.aspx.

16. Elisabeth Babcock, "This Is Your Brain on Stress," *US Partnership on Mobility from Poverty* (blog), October 24, 2016, https://www.mobilitypartnership.org/blog/your-brain-stress.

17. See, for instance, Suniya S. Luthar, Dante Cicchetti, and Bronwyn Becker, "The Construct of Resilience: A Critical Evaluation and Guidelines for Future Work," *Child Development* 71, no. 3 (January 2003): 543–62, doi:10.1111/1467-8624.00164; and Glenn E. Richardson, "The Metatheory of Resilience and Resiliency," *Journal of Clinical Psychology* 58, no. 3 (April 2002): 307–21, doi:10.1002/jclp.10020.

CHAPTER 2

1. Laurence R. Cohen, "I Ain't So Smart, and You Ain't So Dumb: Personal Reassessment in Transformative Learning," *New Directions for Adult & Continuing Education* 1997, no. 74 (Summer 1997): 62, doi:10.1002/ace.7407.

2. In Mezirow's terms, the teacher's expectations for the student to think critically deeply challenged her epistemic meaning perspectives in that she could not conceive of herself as someone who generates knowledge; for her, knowledge is something created by others and received by her. (This, by the way, is a great example of the "received knowing" stage of the *Women's Ways of Knowing* model of development. See Mary Field Belenky, Blythe McVicker Clinchy, Nancy Rule Goldberger, and Jill Mattuck Tarule, *Women's Ways of Knowing: The Development of Self, Voice, and Mind* (New York: Basic Books, 1986).)

3. These experiences encompass Mezirow's first four phases of the transformational learning process.

4. See Jack Mezirow, "A Transformation Theory of Adult Learning," *Annual Adult Education Research Conference (AERC) Proceedings* (Thirty-first, Athens, GA, May 18–20, 1990): 144.

5. M. Carolyn Clark, "Changing Course: Initiating the Transformational Learning Process," *Annual Adult Education Research Conference (AERC) Proceedings* (Thirty-fourth, University Park, PA, May, 1993): 78–83.

6. Chad D. Hoggan, "Insights from Breast Cancer Survivors: The Interplay Between Context, Epistemology, and Change," *Adult Education Quarterly* 64, no. 3 (February 2014): 191–205, doi:10.1177/0741713614523666.

7. Kaye L. A. Yadusky, "Succeeding Against the Odds: Exploring the Experiences of Academically Underprepared College Students Who Successfully Transition from Pre-curriculum Studies to Full Enrollment in Curriculum Courses" (PhD diss., North Carolina State University, 2018).

8. We are not the first to talk about the challenges of developmental education, of course. For an overview of ideas that are being talked about and now being piloted in some community colleges, see Nikki Edgecombe and Susan Bickerstaff, "Addressing Academic Underpreparedness in Service of College Completion," *Texas Education Review* 6, no. 1 (April 2018): 75–83, doi:10.15781/T27941B74.

9. See Jennifer Garvey Berger, "Dancing on the Threshold of Meaning: Recognizing and Understanding the Growing Edge," *Journal of Transformative Education* 2, no. 4 (October 2004): 338, doi:10.1177/1541344604267697.

10. Kaisu Mälkki and Larry Green, "Navigational Aids: The Phenomenology of Transformative Learning," *Journal of Transformative Education* 12, no. 1 (2014): 13, doi:10.1177/1541344614541171.

11. Sue M. Scott, "The Grieving Soul in the Transformation Process," *New Directions for Adult & Continuing Education*, no. 74 (Summer 1997): 41–50, doi:10.1002/ace.7405.

12. Mary Anderson, Jane Goodman, and Nancy Schlossberg, *Counseling Adults in Transition: Linking Schlossberg's Theory with Practice in a Diverse World* (New York: Springer Publishing Company, 2011).

13. These students work under the collective clinical supervision of doctoral students, site supervisors, and NC State faculty.

14. For more information on the model that NC State uses to guide their partnerships such as this, see Marc A. Grimmett et al., "The Community Counseling, Education, and Research Center (CCERC) Model: Addressing Community Mental Health Needs Through Engagement Scholarship," *Journal of Higher Education Outreach & Engagement* 22, no. 3 (2018): 201–30, http://openjournals.libs.uga.edu/index.php/jheoe/article/viewFile/2138/1116.

15. Stephen D. Brookfield, "Overcoming Impostorship, Cultural Suicide, and Lost Innocence: Implications for Teaching Critical Thinking in the Community College," *New Directions for Community Colleges*, no. 130 (Summer 2005): 49–57, doi:10.1002/cc.195.

16. Chad D. Hoggan, "A Typology of Transformation: Reviewing the Transformative Learning Literature," *Studies in the Education of Adults* 48, no. 1 (May 2016): 65–82, doi:10.1080/02660830.2016.1155849.

17. Brookfield, "Overcoming Impostorship, Cultural Suicide, and Lost Innocence," 51.

18. Brookfield, 51.

19. Robert Kegan, "What 'Form' Transforms? A Constructive-Developmental Approach to Transformative Learning," in *Contemporary Theories of Learning*, ed. Knud Illeris (London: Routledge, 2009), 18.

20. See for instance: Claude M. Steele, Steven J. Spencer, and Joshua Aronson, "Contending with Group Image: The Psychology of Stereotype and Social Identity Threat," in *Advances in Experimental Social Psychology* 34, ed. Mark P. Zanna (San Diego: Academic Press, 2002), 379–440; and J. C. Turner et al., *Rediscovering the Social Group: A Self-Categorization Theory* (Oxford: Blackwell, 1987).

21. Mary C. Murphy, Claude M. Steele, and James J. Gross, "Signaling Threat: How Situational Cues Affect Women in Math, Science, and Engineering Settings," *Psychological Science* 18, no. 10 (October 2007): 879–85, doi:10.1111/j.1467-9280.2007 .01995.x.

22. Christine Logel et al., "Interacting with Sexist Men Triggers Social Identity Threat Among Female Engineers," *Journal of Personality and Social Psychology* 96, no. 6 (June 2009): 1089–103, doi:10.1037/a0015703; Sapna Cheryan et al., "Ambient Belonging: How Stereotypical Cues Impact Gender Participation in Computer Science," *Journal of Personality and Social Psychology* 97, no. 6 (December 2009): 1045–60, doi:10.1037/a0016239.

23. Gregory M. Walton et al., "Mere Belonging: The Power of Social Connections," *Journal of Personality and Social Psychology* 102, no. 3 (March 2012): 513–32, doi:10.1037/a0025731.

24. Linden West, "Transformative Learning and the Form That Transforms: Towards a Psychosocial Theory of Recognition Using Auto/Biographical Narrative Research," *Journal of Transformative Education* 12, no. 2 (May 2014): 168, doi:10.1177 /1541344614536054.

25. West, 168.

26. Matt Helmer, "Helping Adult Learners Navigate Community College and the Labor Market," *Courses to Employment Update* 4 (Washington, DC: Aspen Institute, March 2013): 11, https://www.aspeninstitute.org/publications/helping-adult -learners-navigate-community-college-labor-market/.

27. Susan Scrivener et al., *Executive Summary, Doubling Graduation Rates: Three-Year Effects of CUNY's Accelerated Study in Associate Programs (ASAP) for Developmental Education Students* (New York: MDRC, 2015), https://www.mdrc.org/sites/default /files/doubling_graduation_rates_es.pdf.

28. Brookfield provides numerous examples and recommendations, including what we describe here, in Stephen D. Brookfield, *Teaching for Critical Thinking: Tools and Techniques to Help Students Question Their Assumptions* (San Francisco: Jossey-Bass, 2012).

CHAPTER 3

1. Training Futures had two sites at this time. NOVA's President, Bob Templin, made the announcement at a graduation event for one cohort, and the staff announced the news the following day to the cohort at the other site, who were partway through the program.

2. These experiences align with the fifth, sixth, and seventh phases of Mezirow's model.

3. Thomas R. Bailey, D. Timothy Leinbach, and Davis Jenkins, *Is Student Success Labeled Institutional Failure? Student Goals and Graduation Rates in the Accountability Debate at Community Colleges* (CCRC Working Paper No. 1, New York: Columbia University, Teachers College, Community College Research Center, 2006), 20, https://ccrc.tc.columbia.edu/media/k2/attachments/student-success-goals-graduation-rates.pdf.

4. Elizabeth Kopko, Marisol Ramos, and Melinda Karp, *Why Do Some Community College Students Use Institutional Resources Differently Than Others in Program Selection and Planning?* (CCRC Working Paper No. 101, New York: Columbia University, Teachers College, Community College Research Center, 2018), 4, https://ccrc.tc.columbia.edu/media/k2/attachments/why-do-community-college-students-use-institutional-resources-differently.pdf.

5. Anthony P. Carnevale et al., *African Americans: College Majors and Earnings* (Washington, DC: Georgetown University Center on Education and the Workforce, 2016), https://cew.georgetown.edu/wp-content/uploads/AfricanAmericanMajors_2016_web.pdf.

6. Carnevale.

7. Martha C. Nussbaum, *Cultivating Humanity: A Classical Defense of Reform in Liberal Education* (Cambridge, MA: Harvard University Press, 1997), 8–9.

8. Tetyana Kloubert, "Propaganda as a (New) Challenge of Civic Education," *European Journal for Research on the Education and Learning of Adults* 9, no. 2 (2018): 149, doi:10.3384/rela.2000-7426.ojs257.

9. Kopko, Ramos, and Karp, *Why Do Some Community College Students Use Institutional Resources Differently*, 5.

10. Matt Helmer and Amy Blair, *Initial Education and Employment Outcomes Findings for Students Enrolled in the General Services Technician Program 2006–2009* (Washington, DC: Aspen Institute, 2010), http://www.aspenwsi.org/wordpress/wp-content/uploads/10-016.pdf.

11. This term was coined by Hazel Markus and Paula Nurius, "Possible Selves," *American Psychologist* 41, no. 9 (September 1986): 954–69, doi:10.1037/0003-066X.41.9.954, but credit for the application to community college students should be given to Melinda M. Karp, *Toward a New Understanding of Non-Academic Student Support: Four Mechanisms Encouraging Positive Student Outcomes in the Community College* (CCRC Working Paper No. 28, New York: Columbia University, Teachers College, Community College Research Center, 2011), https://files.eric.ed.gov/fulltext/ED516148.pdf.

12. Karp, *Toward a New Understanding of Non-Academic Student Support,* 11.

13. Karp, *Toward a New Understanding of Non-Academic Student Support,* 11.

14. Karp, *Toward a New Understanding of Non-Academic Student Support,* 14.

15. Also, there is no reason why individual colleges should have to create their own vignettes. Regional colleges can work together to create a shared library of video vignettes. For that matter, all the colleges in a state or in the country could create a repository of videos.

16. Kopko, Ramos, and Karp, *Why Do Some Community College Students Use Institutional Resources Differently.*

17. Bailey, Leinbach, and Jenkins, *Is Student Success Labeled Institutional Failure?* 25, 39.

18. For instance, using a multivariate analysis of survey results that tracked 1,080 students over a six-year period, Bailey, Leinbach, and Jenkins found that—after controlling for personal characteristics—students with more ambitious goals enjoyed higher graduation, transfer, and persistence rates. Students who, at their initial intake into community college, expressed the expectation of obtaining a bachelor's degree had a 15 percentage point higher probability of doing so than their peers who did not expect to receive a degree.

19. Davis Jenkins et al., *What We Are Learning about Guided Pathways. Part 1: A Reform Moves from Theory to Practice* (New York: Columbia University, Teachers College, Community College Research Center, 2018), 5, https://ccrc.tc.columbia.edu /media/k2/attachments/guided-pathways-part-1-theory-practice.pdf.

20. VIEW is Virginia's program acronym for TANF, or Temporary Assistance for Needy Families welfare benefits.

21. Judith Scott-Clayton, *The Shapeless River: Does a Lack of Structure Inhibit Students' Progress at Community Colleges?* (CCRC Working Paper No. 25, New York: Columbia University, Teachers College, Community College Research Center, 2011), 1, https://ccrc.tc.columbia.edu/media/k2/attachments/shapeless-river.pdf.

22. Scott-Clayton, 1.

23. Scott-Clayton, 1.

24. Vincent Tinto, *Leaving College: Rethinking the Causes and Cures of Student Attrition* (Chicago: University of Chicago Press, 1993); James Rosenbaum, Regina Deil-Amen, and Ann Person, *After Admission: From College Access to College Success* (New York: Russell Sage Foundation, 2006).

25. Thomas R. Bailey, Shanna S. Jaggars, and Davis Jenkins, *Redesigning America's Community Colleges: A Clearer Path to Student Success* (Cambridge, MA: Harvard University Press, 2015).

26. This argument is based on and credited to Regina Deil-Amen and James E. Rosenbaum, "The Social Prerequisites of Success: Can College Structure Reduce the Need for Social Know-How?" *The ANNALS of the American Academy of Political and Social Science* 586, no. 1 (March 2003): 120–43, doi:10.1177/0002716202250216.

27. We recognize that this design philosophy is called by many different names. We use "guided pathways" because it is a term used across the country, whereas most other terms are used only in a particular state or an individual community college.

28. Jan Meyer, Ray Land, and Caroline Baillie, eds., *Threshold Concepts and Transformational Learning* (Rotterdam: Sense Publishers, 2010).

29. Jan Meyer and Ray Land, *Threshold Concepts and Troublesome Knowledge: Linkages to Ways of Thinking and Practising Within the Disciplines* (Edinburgh: School of Education, University of Edinburgh, 2003), 4–5, https://www.colorado.edu/ftep /sites/default/files/attached-files/meyer_and_land_-_threshold_concepts.pdf.

30. Brent Orrell, "STEM without Fruit: How Noncognitive Skills Improve Workforce Outcomes," AEI paper studies (2018).

31. Jean Lave, Michael Murtaugh, and Olivia de la Rocha, "The Dialectic of Arithmetic in Grocery Shopping," in *Everyday Cognition: Its Development in Social Context*, ed. Barbara Rogoff and Jean Lave (Cambridge, MA: Harvard University Press, 1984), 67–94, http://hci.ucsd.edu/102b/readings/Lave.PDF.

32. Arthur L. Wilson, "The Promise of Situated Cognition," *New Directions for Adult & Continuing Education*, no. 57 (Spring 1993): 74, doi:10.1002/ace.36719935709.

33. John S. Brown, Allan Collins, and Paul Duguid, "Situated Cognition and the Culture of Learning," *Educational Researcher* 18, no. 1 (January 1989): 35, doi:10.3102/0013189X018001032.

34. Karp, *Toward a New Understanding of Non-Academic Student Support*, 11.

CHAPTER 4

1. These experiences encompass the eighth, ninth, and tenth phases of Mezirow's model of the transformational learning process.

2. Rebecca S. Wheeler, "Becoming Adept at Code-Switching," *Educational Leadership* 65, no. 7 (April 2008): 54–58, http://www.ascd.org/publications/educational_leadership/apr08/vol65/num07/Becoming_Adept_at_Code-Switching.aspx.

3. BEV as a legitimate dialect was established by researchers in the 1960s and 1970s. See, for instance, Robbins Burling, *English in Black and White* (New York: Holt, Rinehart and Winston, Inc., 1973) and also William Labov, *Language in the Inner City: Studies in the Black English Vernacular* (Philadelphia: University of Pennsylvania Press, 1972). It is now also called African American Vernacular English (AAVE).

4. See Amanda J. Godley et al., "Preparing Teachers for Dialectally Diverse Classrooms," *Educational Researcher* 35, no. 8 (November 2006): 30–37, https://pdfs.semanticscholar.org/79b4/c87f2969a14e444d95e01eabaf2d38d3879e.pdf, and Sonia Nieto, *Affirming Diversity: The Sociopolitical Context of Multicultural Education*, 3rd ed. (New York: Longman, 2000).

5. Rebecca S. Wheeler, "What Do We Do About Student Grammar—All Those Missing ed's and s's? Using Comparison and Contrast to Teach Standard English in Dialectally Diverse Classrooms," *English Teaching: Practice and Critique* 5, no. 1 (May 2006): 16–33, https://files.eric.ed.gov/fulltext/EJ843817.pdf.

6. Wheeler, "Becoming Adept at Code-Switching," 57.

7. Susan Craver, email to authors, Dec 29, 2018.

8. Gisela S. Vélez and Gabriela R. Giner, "Effects of Business Internships on Students, Employers, and Higher Education Institutions: A Systematic Review," *Journal of Employment Counseling* 52, no. 3 (September 2015): 121–30, doi:10.1002/joec.12010.

9. George D. Kuh, *High-Impact Educational Practices: What They Are, Who Has Access to Them, and Why They Matter* (Washington, DC: Association of American Colleges & Universities, 2008).

10. From a January 24, 2019, national webinar presentation (and prior conference presentations) delivered by Julie Parks, executive director of Workforce Training at Grand Rapids Community College, MI.

11. Manfred F. R. Kets de Vries, "The Dangers of Feeling Like a Fake," *Harvard Business Review* 83, no. 9 (September 2005): 110.

12. This is an abridged version of the definition offered on dictionary.com

13. Pauline R. Clance and Suzanne A. Imes, "The Impostor Phenomenon in High Achieving Women: Dynamics and Therapeutic Intervention," *Psychotherapy Theory, Research and Practice* 15, no. 3 (Fall 1978): 241–47, doi:10.1037/h0086006.

14. Rose O. Sherman, "Imposter Syndrome: When You Feel Like You're Faking It," *American Nurse Today* 8, no. 5 (May 2013): 57.

15. Stephen D. Brookfield, "Overcoming Impostorship, Cultural Suicide, and Lost Innocence: Implications for Teaching Critical Thinking in the Community College," *New Directions for Community Colleges*, no. 130 (Summer 2005): 51, doi:10.1002/cc.195.

16. Nancy K. Schlossberg, "Marginality and Mattering: Key Issues in Building Community," *New Directions for Student Services*, no. 48 (Winter 1989): 5–15, doi:10.1002/ss.37119894803.

17. Anna Weigand Parkman, "The Imposter Phenomenon in Higher Education: Incidence and Impact," *Journal of Higher Education Theory and Practice* 16, no. 1 (2016): 51, http://www.na-businesspress.com/JHETP/ParkmanA_Web16_1_.pdf.

18. Mary E. H. Topping, "The Impostor Phenomenon : A Study of Its Construct and Incidence in University Faculty Members" (PhD diss., University of South Florida, 1983).

19. Queena Hoang, "The Impostor Phenomenon: Overcoming Internalized Barriers and Recognizing Achievements," *The Vermont Connection* 34, no. 1 (2013): 42–51, https://scholarworks.uvm.edu/tvc/vol34/iss1/6/. Note: Hoang's focus was on graduate students. However, we believe her conclusions are also applicable to community college students.

20. See Robert Kegan, *The Evolving Self: Problem and Process in Human Development* (Cambridge, MA: Harvard University Press, 1983), and Nevitt Sanford, *Self & Society: Social Change and Individual Development* (New York: Atherton, 1966).

21. Albert Bandura, "Self-Efficacy: Toward a Unifying Theory of Behavioral Change," *Psychological Review* 84, no. 2 (1977): 191–215, doi:10.1037/0033-295X.84.2.191.

22. Vincent Tinto, *Leaving College: Rethinking the Causes and Cures of Student Attrition* (Chicago: University of Chicago Press, 1993).

23. Laura I. Rendón, Romero E. Jalomo, and Amaury Nora, "Theoretical Considerations in the Study of Minority Student Retention in Higher Education," in *Reworking the Student Departure Puzzle*, John M. Braxton, ed. (Nashville, TN: Vanderbilt University, 2000), 127–56.

24. Matt Helmer and Amy Blair, *Initial Education and Employment Outcomes Findings for Students Enrolled in Healthcare Career Training 2003–2009* (Washington, DC: Aspen Institute, 2011), http://www.aspenwsi.org/wordpress/wp-content/uploads/10-015.pdf.

25. Thomas R. Bailey, Dong Wook Jeong, and Sung-Woo Cho, *Student Progression Through Developmental Sequences in Community Colleges* (CCRC Brief No. 45, New York: Columbia University, Teachers College, Community College Research Center, 2010), https://ccrc.tc.columbia.edu/media/k2/attachments/student-progression-through-developmental-sequences-brief.pdf.

26. Paul Tough, "Who Gets to Graduate," *New York Times Magazine*, May 15, 2014, https://www.nytimes.com/2014/05/18/magazine/who-gets-to-graduate.html.

27. Dave Paunesku et al., *Changing Mindsets to Raise Achievement: The Stanford University Project for Education Research That Scales (PERTS)* (Stanford: PERTS, 2014), https://www.westada.org/cms/lib/ID01904074/Centricity/Domain/209/University%20and%20Partner%20Research/PERTS_Summary_February_2014.pdf.

28. Vincent Tinto, *Completing College: Rethinking Institutional Action* (Chicago: University of Chicago Press, 2012), 54.

29. For rationales behind and suggestions for designing formative assessments, see Brent Duckor, "Formative Assessment in Seven Good Moves," *Educational Leadership* 71, no. 6 (March 2014): 28–32, https://www.greatschoolspartnership.org/wp-content/uploads/2016/11/Formative-Assessment-in-Seven-Good-Moves.pdf.

30. Marcia B. Baxter Magolda, "Self-Authorship as the Common Goal of 21st-Century Education," in *Learning Partnerships: Theory and Models of Practice to Educate for Self-Authorship,* Marcia B. Baxter Magolda and Patricia M. King, eds. (Sterling, VA: Stylus, 2004), 1–35.

31. Aneeta Rattan, Catherine Good, and Carol S. Dweck, "It's Ok—Not Everyone Can be Good at Math": Instructors with an Entity Theory Comfort (and Demotivate) Students," *Journal of Experimental Social Psychology* 48, no. 3 (May 2012): 731–37.

32. For an overview of the Imaginal Education model used at Training Futures (published by the Aspen Institute), see http://www.aspenwsi.org/wordpress/wp-content/uploads/ImaginalEducationOverview.pdf.

33. Knud Illeris, "Transformative Learning and Identity," *Journal of Transformative Education* 12, no. 2 (September 2014): 155.

34. Hazel Markus and Paula Nurius, "Possible Selves," *American Psychologist* 41, no. 9 (September 1986): 954–69, doi:10.1037/0003-066X.41.9.954.

35. Mark Tennant, *The Learning Self: Understanding the Potential for Transformation* (San Francisco: Jossey-Bass, 2012).

36. Ai-Jen Poo and Eldar Shafir, "Changing the Narrative," *US Partnership on Mobility from Poverty* (blog), 2018, https://www.mobilitypartnership.org/changing-narrative.

37. Technically, we should use the term "conceptual metaphors," as we mean to include similes and analogies in addition to metaphors (strictly defined).

38. For one of the definitive texts on meaning-making, see George Lakoff and Mark Johnson, *Metaphors We Live By* (Chicago: University of Chicago Press, 1980). For further reading on metaphors and change, see David Deshler, "Metaphor Analysis: Exorcising Social Ghosts" in *Fostering Critical Reflection in Adulthood: A Guide to*

Transformative and Emancipatory Learning, Jack Mezirow and associates (San Francisco: Jossey-Bass, 1990), 296–313; John Dirkx, "Nurturing Soul Work: A Jungian Approach to Transformative Learning" in *The Handbook of Transformative Learning: Theory, Research, and Practice,* ed. Edward W. Taylor and Patricia Cranton (San Francisco: Jossey-Bass, 2012), 116–30; Chad Hoggan, Soni Simpson, and Heather Stuckey, eds., *Creative Expression in Transformative Learning: Tools and Techniques for Educators of Adults* (Malabar, FL: Krieger, 2009).

39. Chad D. Hoggan, "Transformative Learning Through Conceptual Metaphors: Simile, Metaphor, and Analogy as Levers for Learning." *Adult Learning* 25, no. 4 (2014): 134–41, doi:10.1177/1045159514546215. Of note in this article is that after these findings were created, the author discovered they were consistent with those from a meta-review of the literature of another discipline.

40. Chad D. Hoggan, Kaisu Mälkki, and Fergal Finnegan, "Developing the Theory of Perspective Transformation: Continuity, Intersubjectivity, and Emancipatory Praxis," *Adult Education Quarterly* 67, no. 1 (2016): 51–52, doi:10.1177/0741713616674076.

41. Maureen Conway, Linda Dworak, and Allison Gerber, *Beyond Graduation: Promoting Post-Program Engagement and Advancement* (Washington, DC: Aspen Institute, 2001).

CHAPTER 5

1. We acknowledge that the increases cannot be attributed to specific changes in practices, and some level of employment increase would have been expected even in the absence of the leadership program.

2. You can use Pell grant awardees as a proxy to identify low-income students.

3. For an example of the NOVA–Training Futures project plan, see http://www.aspenwsi.org/wordpress/wp-content/uploads/Training-Futures-Project-Planning-Tool-Completed-Example.pdf.

4. https://www.achievingthedream.org/

APPENDIX

1. There were two program sites during most of the time frame covered by this book.

2. For an overview of the Imaginal Education model used at Training Futures (published by the Aspen Institute), see http://www.aspenwsi.org/wordpress/wp-content/uploads/ImaginalEducationOverview.pdf.

3. Imaginal Education's use of the term "images" is similar to Transformational Learning's use of "meaning perspectives." We see images as one part of a larger system of meaning perspectives, as the latter also include assumptions, identities, worldviews, and so forth. However, this distinction is not important for the purposes of describing how imaginal education's approach to teaching focuses on the tacit, internal processes of learners.

4. Training Futures had two sites at this time. NOVA's President, Bob Templin, made the announcement at a graduation event for one cohort, and the staff announced

the news the following day to the cohort at the other site, who were partway through the program.

5. For more information about the Aspen Institute's Courses to Employment demonstration project, see www.coursestoemployment.org.

6. Matt Helmer and Amy Blair, *Initial Education and Employment Outcomes Findings for Students Enrolled in Business and Medical Office Administration Training 2007–2010* (Washington, DC: Aspen Institute, 2011), http://www.aspenwsi.org /wordpress/wp-content/uploads/10-044.pdf.

ACKNOWLEDGMENTS

T HE AUTHORS ARE GRATEFUL to several groups of people who helped to shape this book in different ways throughout our two-year development process.

Dr. Robert Templin Jr., former president of Northern Virginia Community College (NOVA), Senior Fellow with the College Excellence Program at the Aspen Institute, and professor of practice in North Carolina State University's College of Education, has been a steady presence throughout this process. The NOVA–Training Futures partnership was one of many community-based partnerships formed at NOVA under his leadership that wove together the assets of the college and nearby organizations to better serve neighbors who might otherwise struggle to afford or succeed in college. Dr. Templin first introduced the two authors in 2015, provided encouragement during the book proposal phase, and served as a reviewer of the initial manuscript.

Susan Craver and Marla Burton, cofounders of Northern Virginia Family Service's Training Futures program, also contributed in many ways during the development of this book. They have continually refined the delivery of the Training Futures "Imaginal Education" transformational learning approach and methods, they shared their insights about the participants' transformational learning processes in a meeting with the authors, and they helped to draft and review the descriptions of those methodologies used in the book. Both Susan and Marla also provided comments and fact-checking guidance in their review of the initial manuscript.

We thank Meredith Archer Hatch, senior associate director at Achieving the Dream, for recommending that the coauthors deliver a conference workshop at the DREAM 2016 conference. The enthusiastic standing-room-only response by over 100 community college attendees at this workshop provided early inspiration and momentum in the collaboration that became this book.

We acknowledge the tremendous help provided by Somanita Kheang and Keith Street Robinson, PhD students at North Carolina State University. They assisted with many technical issues of finding and correcting references, formatting the text, and so forth. We also thank a group of knowledgeable advisors who reviewed a preliminary draft of the manuscript and offered guidance on ways to strengthen the book. They are:

- Susan Barbitta, Executive Director of Student Success, North Carolina Community College System
- Sarah Deal, Associate Director of Special Projects, North Carolina Community College System
- Tonya Ensign, PhD, President, emagine, llc
- Deana Guido, PhD, Associate Vice President of Transfer Initiatives, Nash Community College
- Elizabeth Kasl, PhD, independent scholar
- Tetyana Kloubert, PhD, Professor of Adult Education, Catholic University of Eichstätt-Ingolstadt
- Tracy Mancini, EdD, Vice President of Instruction and Student Support, Carteret Community College
- Julie Mullen, Director of Workforce Development, Northern Virginia Family Service

- Renee Owen, EdD, Executive Director, Rainbow Community School
- Lauren Pellegrino, PhD, Senior Research Associate, Community College Research Center

We are especially grateful to the many Training Futures participants whose stories and quotes are included in this book, along with their peers who shared and supported one another in these collective transformational learning journeys. Their experiences, shared openly and honestly with the cohort and at larger program events, form the heart and soul of the book.

We would also like to extend our gratitude to our editor at Harvard Education Press, Jayne M. Fargnoli. Jayne's combination of support and encouragement, along with her critical review of multiple manuscript drafts, provided the authors with steady direction throughout the two-year process of developing this book from initial concept through final publication.

ABOUT THE AUTHORS

CHAD D. HOGGAN is an associate professor of adult, workforce and continuing professional education in the Department of Educational Leadership, Policy, and Human Development at North Carolina State University in Raleigh, North Carolina. Prior to joining NC State in 2012, he was an instructor of organizational leadership at Wright State University in Dayton, Ohio.

Hoggan's higher education journey began as a dual-enrollment student at Johnson County Community College in Overland Park, Kansas. After transferring to a university and completing a degree in business management, his early career was as a workplace safety trainer and consultant, working with organizations to develop effective safety programs. Yearning to understand more about personal learning and organizational culture change, he enrolled in a graduate program at NC State, where he developed a passion for research around personal, organizational, and social transformation. Hoggan received a master of education in adult and community college education from NC State, and then obtained his Doctor of Education in adult learning and leadership from Teachers College, Columbia University.

Hoggan is the editor of the *Journal of Transformative Education*. His research primarily revolves around transformational learning, which he has studied in a wide range of research contexts: military veterans in community college, higher education students in leadership development courses, and women navigating the psychosocial transition of breast cancer survivorship. A current focus of his research is on the challenges of community college student success. Recently he has also collaborated with the Aspen Institute and faculty at NC State to redesign their doctoral program in community college leadership.

BILL BROWNING is an independent consultant with a thirty-year career combining management roles in corporate training, a community-based nonprofit, community college, and workforce development policy and leadership training.

For the first half of his career, Browning climbed into senior management ranks at the American Bankers Association, becoming managing director of a $4 million, twenty-five-person national corporate training consulting enterprise. Since 2001, he has redeployed his knowledge of adult learning in community-based job training and community leadership development focused on serving low-income, disadvantaged, and minority workers. Browning served for five years as program manager for Northern Virginia Family Service's (NVFS) job training programs for low-income minority adults, which included the Training Futures program as well as a pre-apprenticeship construction training program. While at NVFS, Browning helped to document the Training Futures program's transformational learning program design, and led an innovative coenrollment partnership with Northern Virginia Community College (NOVA) that was recognized by the Aspen Institute as a national model.

For the next six years at NOVA, Browning led college efforts to refine the coenrollment partnership with Training Futures and to forge partnerships with several other high performing nonprofits that train low-income minority workers in multiple business sectors, including Goodwill Industries and Year Up. He also led and launched an Adult Career Pathways initiative that helped 1,000 low-income and mostly minority students access and succeed in college studies at NOVA. At the Aspen Institute, Browning researched and authored several case studies documenting effective workforce development practices at community colleges, managed national and local workforce development leadership training programs, and designed and conducted workshops for numerous national conferences and webinars.

Since becoming an independent consultant in 2016, Browning has worked with national and regional clients to document effective practices, train community college and workforce development leaders, and to help launch innovative new projects. He is based in the Washington, DC, metropolitan region.

INDEX